To: R. Campbell 917764

From: Your friend
Yen Yi Gang
in China

A CONCISE HISTORY OF CHINA

Jian Bozan
Shao Xunzheng Hu Hua

FOREIGN LANGUAGES PRESS
BEIJING

First Edition 1964
Second Edition 1981

Published by the Foreign Languages Press
24 Baiwanzhuang Road, Beijing, China

Printed by the Foreign Languages Printing House
19 West Chegongzhuang Road, Beijing, China

Distributed by Guoji Shudian (China Publications Centre)
P.O. Box 399, Beijing, China

Printed in the People's Republic of China

CONTENTS

MODERN PERIOD
(The Period of the Old Democratic Revolution)

CONTEMPORARY PERIOD
(The Period of the New Democratic Revolution)

INTRODUCTION

This *Concise History of China* was written by the authors in consultation with the Chinese Historical Society.

China is a country with a very early civilization and a long and rich history. The purpose of this book is to give a brief introduction to her history and to outline the development of Chinese society.

The book is in three parts: early, modern and contemporary periods.

Like all other peoples, the Chinese have passed through primitive commune, slave and feudal systems. The development of feudal society in China was a slow and protracted process, the feudal landlord class maintaining itself by extremely ruthless exploitation and oppression of the peasantry. Nevertheless, society did progress, thanks to the continual revolutionary struggles waged by the Chinese peasants. The three large-scale peasant uprisings at the end of the Qin, Sui and Yuan dynasties gave a powerful impetus to the development of the productive forces of society. The Han, Tang and Ming dynasties with their mighty national power and brilliant culture rose on this foundation. Chinese history testifies to the glorious revolutionary traditions of the Chinese people and their splendid historical heritage.

Britain launched the Opium War against China in 1840, and from that time on imperialist forces made continuous inroads into China. Working hand in glove with Chinese feudalism, they hindered the growth of Chinese capitalism and China became a semi-colonial and semi-feudal country. China's capitalist economy went through twists and turns and developed at a slow tempo. With the deeper penetration of the aggressive forces of imperialism into the country, the Chinese people became utterly impoverished, but more determined and powerful in their resistance. The first upsurge of the people's revolution was the Taiping Revolution, launched by the peasants in 1851. It speeded up the collapse of the feudal rule of the Qing Dynasty. The second upsurge was the Yi He Tuan movement launched by the peasants in 1900. During this movement the Chinese people dealt a severe blow at the joint forces of the imperialist powers who were compelled to abandon, for the time being, their schemes for the partitioning of China. The third upsurge was the bourgeois-led 1911 Revolution. It overthrew the feudal monarchy which had reigned for two thousand years in China, and the Provisional Revolutionary Government instituted a provisional constitution. The idea of a democratic republic became embedded in the mind of the people, and restoration of the monarchy was out of the question. However, as the Chinese bourgeoisie was too weak to defeat imperialism and feudalism, it could not change the semi-colonial and semi-feudal character of Chinese society. The history of the Chinese revolution demonstrates that only under the leadership of the working class has it been possible for the Chinese people to really complete the anti-imperialist and anti-feudal revolution.

The salvoes of the 1917 October Socialist Revolution in Russia were echoed by the introduction of Marxism-Leninism into China. The Chinese capitalist economy had then further developed and the Chinese proletariat had become powerful enough to lead the revolution. Under the influence of Marxism-Leninism the May 4th Movement of 1919 started, and a new period in Chinese history was inaugurated, the period of the new democratic revolution. The Chinese Communist Party, founded in 1921, led the entire people to wage resolute struggles against imperialism, feudalism and bureaucrat-capitalism. Rallying round the Communist Party, the Chinese people fought three revolutionary civil wars and the War of Resistance Against Japan, finally bringing about the great victory of the new democratic revolution. The People's Republic of China was founded on October 1, 1949. With the birth of the People's Republic, the greatest world event following the October Revolution, China entered the new era of building socialism.

EARLY PERIOD
(Primitive Society, Slave Society and Feudal Society)

I. REMOTE ANTIQUITY TO THE PERIOD OF THE WARRING STATES (Prior to 300 B.C.)

Archaeological Discoveries Excavations during the last scores of years have established that man has lived for a very long time in the country known as China today. Fossil remains of the early Palaeolithic Ape Man, his stone implements, as well as large quantities of other palaeontological fossils have been found on various occasions since 1929 at Zhoukoudian (Choukoutien), fifty kilometres southwest of Beijing. Studies carried out by experts reveal that the Chinese Ape Man, also known as the Peking Man (*Sinanthropus Pekinensis*), lived in the Pleistocene period of the Quarternary era, about 500,000 years ago. In 1954 fossil human teeth and a large quantity of stone implements belonging to the Middle Palaeolithic Age were found in Dingcun Village, Xiangfen County, Shanxi Province. The fossilized bones of the homo sapiens of the Late Palaeolithic Age (now known as the Upper Cave Man) and large quantities of stone implements and bone artifacts were unearthed in an upper cave on the Dragon Bone Hill at Zhoukoudian in 1934. In addition, fossil remains of human beings and objects of the Palaeolithic Age have also been discovered in Maba of Shaoguan in Guangdong, Changyang in Hubei, Liujiang in Guangxi and the Hetao (Yellow River Bend) region.

Neolithic remains distributed over an extensive area have been discovered in many parts of China.

The finds include painted and black pottery and small stone implements, belonging to the period between the Palaeolithic and Neolithic Ages. Specimens of painted pottery (also known as Yangshao culture) have been unearthed in an area extending from modern Henan, Shanxi and Shaanxi to Gansu. Specimens of black pottery (also known as Longshan culture) have also been unearthed over a wide area, mainly in Shandong Province and the central plains. Evidence of Microlithic culture has been found in regions north of the Great Wall, and evidence of Neolithic culture of the south China type has been discovered in many areas south of the Changjiang (Yangtse) River.

Prehistoric Legends Prehistoric legends and characters abound in the ancient books of China. The most notable of the legendary figures are: Huang Di (the Yellow Emperor) who used jade to make weapons with which to conquer other tribes; Lei Zu, his wife, who introduced the rearing of silkworms; Shun, the inventor of lacquerware; and Yu, or the Great Yu, who used bronze weapons to vanquish the Miao people and who harnessed great floods. Society, as reflected in these legends, was based on the primitive commune in which classes, private property and exploitation of man by man were unknown.

Xia (About 21st to 17th Century B.C.) and Shang (About 17th to 11th Century B.C.) According to tradition the Xia Dynasty was the first Chinese dynasty that ruled a state. The Great Yu, King of Xia, was succeeded by his son Qi, and his descendants. The Xia Dynasty ended with its last king, Jie. It was overthrown by Shang.

Written records of the Shang or Yin Dynasty,[1] made by contemporaries, still exist. Some of the writings of this period were cast in bronze, some inscribed on tortoise shells or animal bones. Shang bronzes have been unearthed during a number of successive dynasties. Archaeologists have carried out further excavations in recent years in Anyang County, Henan, and have found an abundance of them. The ruins of an early Yin city and a large number of Yin cultural relics unearthed at Zhengzhou show that the city must have also been a centre for Yin culture. Oracle bones were first discovered in 1899 at Xiaotun Village, Anyang, on the Ruins of Yin. Since 1899 large quantities of oracle bones have been unearthed. Expert studies show that they record revelations made by contemporary diviners about various events.

Some rudimentary knowledge of Shang culture has been obtained from this wealth of material.

First, the discovery of an extraordinary variety of Shang bronzes shows that production had reached the bronze age. The specimens include cutlery, kitchen utensils, drinking vessels and weapons of war. The "Si Mu Wu Ding", a large tripod weighing 1,400 catties (700 kilogrammes), is a magnificent work of art. The sheer grace of small bronzes such as spoons, wine cups and arrow heads is a delight to the eye. These bronzes are outstanding among world examples of bronze culture for their

---

[1] King Pangeng of Shang moved his capital to Yin and the Shang Dynasty was thereafter known as the Yin Dynasty.

number, variety of shape, skilful workmanship, and beauty of design.

Second, the discoveries provide evidence that the Shang Dynasty had entered into the stage of agriculture. Oracle inscriptions contain many records of divinations of harvests and rainfall, indicating that farming occupied an important place in the life of the people. Glutinous millet is the farm product most frequently mentioned in the inscriptions. Wheat comes next. It may be presumed that these two kinds of grain were the most common staple grains of the time. From the frequent references to "silkworm", "mulberry tree", and "silk" and "silk cloth", we know that the nobles used silk for clothing. Cattle-herding had by this time been relegated to a secondary position. The animals domesticated were much the same as those in present-day use — horses, cattle, sheep, dogs and pigs, all being mentioned in the inscriptions. The Shang people used horses and cattle as draught-animals for their chariots and carts. Elephants existed in the Huanghe (Yellow) River valley at the time and were used in war. These facts are confirmed by archaeological discoveries and inscriptions on oracle bones.

Third, these remains also indicate that Shang society was a slave society. The advanced quality of the unearthed bronzes implies that there must have been officials in charge of large numbers of slave-craftsmen engaged in the creation of luxury articles for the use of the nobles. There is also evidence of the existence of many diviners, who offered sacrifices and engaged in divination and in the writing and inscribing of the revelations. The craftsmen and diviners must obviously have been relieved from the production of bare necessities in order to carry out their special work. From this it may be deduced that a large number of people must have been employed in agriculture and stock-raising to provide the means of subsistence for those not engaged in production.

Another fact pointing to the existence of slavery during the Shang Dynasty is the remains of a number of people, obviously buried as sacrifices in the tombs of the nobles, three or even four hundred having been discovered in a single grave. Over two thousand human sacrifices were found in excavated tombs on the Ruins of Yin, an indication that the total number of slaves must have been very high. It can be assumed that they were either prisoners of war or offenders. Historical sources show that in the Shang State wars were of frequent occurrence and that punishment was severe.

From material available at present it is impossible to define the exact territorial limits of the Shang domain, but it is known that its people were active over a very large area. Roughly speaking, the Shang rule in the north extended over the central part of what is now Hebei, the Changjiang and Huaihe rivers and Hubei in the south, Shandong in the east and Shaanxi in the west. Within this vast region numerous tribes and petty states paid homage to the Shang rulers.

The names of the rulers of the Shang Dynasty are to be found in the "Chronicle of Yin" in Sima Qian's *Historical Records.* It names thirteen generations from Xie, the first eminent ruler of the Shang people, to King Tang, who founded the Shang Dynasty. Between Tang and the last Shang ruler, King Zhou, there was a total of thirty kings. The names of these kings as recorded in the "Chronicle of Yin" agree in general with those inscribed on the oracle bones.

The duration of the Shang Dynasty has not yet been established with certainty. According to the *Commentary on Confucius' Spring and Autumn Annals by Zuo Qiu-ming,* it had a history of 600 years.

Western Zhou (About 11th Century to 771 B.C.) and Eastern Zhou (770-221 B.C.) The Zhou people in the Wei River valley in Shanxi rose in revolt during the closing years of the Shang Dynasty. No exact dates have been established for the period during which the Zhou Dynasty began to establish itself and finally overthrew the Shang Dynasty. According to traditional accounts, Western Zhou conquered Shang in the late 11th century B.C. The "Chronological Table of Twelve Princes" contained in the *Historical Records* starts with the year 841 B.C., and it is from that year that the history of China is accurately dated.

Early Zhou ballads and songs record that the first ruler of the house of Zhou was Qi, the son of a mythical being named Jiang Yuan. Qi was said to be the first to cultivate panicled millet, a type much easier to grow than glutinous millet, which replaced the latter as the staple food of the people. This was a great contribution and Qi became revered as the god of agriculture and honoured with the title of Hou Ji (Lord Cultivator).

Tradition claims that the Zhou people flourished in the region of Tai (Wugong County in present-day Shaanxi Province). Remains found in the Wei River valley have been identified as belonging to the Zhou period. The areas around Qishan (in Western Shaanxi Province), and Feng and Hao, both near present-day Xian, abound with relics of the Zhou people.

After the Zhou people had migrated several times and their leader Tai Wang had moved to "Zhou's Plain", i.e., present-day Qishan County, they gradually became strong and adopted Zhou as the name of their territory. Wang Ji, the son of Tai Wang, became a powerful ruler, but he was subsequently killed by Wen Ding, the king of Shang. The oracle inscriptions indicate that Zhou had once been a vassal state of Shang.

King Wen, the son of Wang Ji, conquered the neighbouring petty states and united the whole of the Wei River valley under his rule. He then moved his capital to Feng (near present-day Xian) on the lower reaches of the Wei River, and his authority extended to what are now Shanxi and Henan provinces. His son, King Wu, overthrew Shang, founded the Zhou Dynasty, and moved the capital from Feng to Haojing (also near present-day Xian). Because the new dynasty established its seat of government at a place to the west of Luoyi to which the house of Zhou later moved, historians refer to it as Western Zhou.

After King Wu's death the Shang people rose in revolt. Zhou Gong, Duke of Zhou and brother of King Wu, launched a big expedition eastwards. During the course of the expedition he conquered more than fifty states, wiped out all vestiges of Shang power in the east, and extended Zhou rule to the lower reaches of the Huanghe River valley.

To consolidate the rule of Zhou, the Duke of Zhou handed over the newly conquered lands and the people there to the nobles of the house of Zhou and also to some other nobles. The sons of King Wen, King Wu and Zhou Gong and others of the same royal house were made princes and princelings and granted fiefs in the territory of the present-day provinces of Shanxi, Henan, Shandong, Shaanxi, Hebei and Hubei. Most of the fiefs were in Henan. Tradition claims that Zhou Gong created seventy-one principalities. Numerous petty states were also conquered by Zhou. As vassals, these states obeyed the decrees of Zhou and rendered tribute to its rulers.

The stage of development of Western Zhou society is still a matter of controversy among Chinese historians. Many see it as an incipient stage of feudalism, while others maintain that it was still a slave society. Modern archaeological research and extant records reveal the following characteristics of Western Zhou society:

(1) The social productive forces under Western Zhou were more developed than those under Shang. This is shown primarily in the development of agricultural production. The inscriptions on bronzes and the records contained in the *Book of Songs* and the *Book of History* indicate that Western Zhou was already a prosperous agricultural society. Improved farming implements, greater variety of agricultural products and an enlarged scale of agriculture show that under Western Zhou the productive level was higher than under the previous dynasty. It can be stated that superior agriculture prevailed wherever Western Zhou rule extended, and that the Zhou people made a notable contribution to the development of the Huanghe River valley.

(2) The relations of social production in this period were a definite advance on those under Shang. Inscriptions on bronzes and records contained in the *Book of Songs* and the *Book of History* provide evidence of the existence of a hierarchy based on the private ownership of land. The king made gifts of land and of the people on it to his princes, who in turn granted part of this land and its people to their own ministers. A class of landowners who owned the people on the land thus arose.

The position of those who actually cultivated the land and did not own it was in sharp contrast to this class. They were scarcely allowed the use of enough land to raise a bare minimum of food for their families and had to till the lands of the king, the princes, and the ministers without remuneration. These direct tillers of the soil did not receive their means of subsistence from the landowners, and had their own instruments of production, houses, and vegetable gardens. The landowners retained proprietary rights over their persons.

(3) The hierarchical system of Western Zhou was closely connected with the patriarchal system, which established the right of succession by the eldest son. Title and property were inherited by the first son born by the legal wife. This eldest son, heir to the title and estate of his father, was called *zong zi* (heir apparent). The king of Zhou was the *zong zi* of the kingdom. The prince was the *zong zi* of a state, and the minister was the *zong zi* of his family. These *zong zi*, of different political ranks, were actually landowners with holdings of different sizes.

(4) Western Zhou culture was a development of Shang's. This fact is apparent both from its artistic creations and from the form of the ideographs used in the writing of that period. The odes and songs in the *Book of Songs* and the orders of conferment and chronicles in the *Book of History* are more advanced, in the literary sense, than those of Shang. Many inscriptions on bronze, several hundred words in length, dating back to the later Western Zhou period, still survive. The Zhou people also had a more elaborated conception of natural and supernatural powers.

The last ruler of Western Zhou was King You. He

was killed by Quan Rong, a western tribe, and his son, King Ping, moved the capital from Haojing eastwards to the city of Luoyi (present-day Luoyang in Henan Province) in 770 B.C., the year when Eastern Zhou rule started. The period from 772 B.C. to 481 B.C. is known as the Spring and Autumn, while that from 403 B.C. to 221 B.C. is known as the Warring States. During the five centuries of the rule of Eastern Zhou, Chinese culture registered brilliant achievements and made great progress.

Social conditions under Eastern Zhou during the Spring and Autumn and Warring States periods made a marked advance in comparison with those under Western Zhou. Here are some of their characteristics:

1. The discovery and use of iron promoted the growth of the productive forces of society. The earliest mention of iron in authentic Chinese documents is that the 513 B.C. legal code of the state of Jin was cast in relief on an iron tripod, indicating that China was making cast iron as early as the late sixth century B.C. In the late Spring and Autumn Period and in the Warring States Period, iron was much more widely used, as shown by archaeological finds. Large numbers of iron moulds were unearthed in Xinglong County, Hebei Province, and iron tools and weapons were also found in graves dating back to the Warring States Period in Huixian County, Henan Province.

The discovery of iron made it possible to produce more and better farm and handicraft tools, with the result that both agriculture and handicraft improved. This in turn stimulated trading activities and the castles of the princes began to develop into cities and towns. During the Warring States Period, towns with a population of ten thousand households became quite common. For example, Linzi, the capital of the state of Qi (modern Shandong), boasted a population of seventy thousand households. It is recorded that there was an incessant flow of carriages along the highways day and night in the state of Wei (modern Henan) — testimonies to the prosperity and affluence of the time.

A means of exchange arises when trade reaches a certain stage of development. There is a long history of the use of money in China, but it was not until the time of the Warring States that metal tokens came into general use. Many trading centres of that period minted their own metal tokens. The existence of more than two hundred of these centres has been verified.

2. With the development of the productive forces, changes in landownership began to take place. The aristocracy had held all the land since the time of Western Zhou, and trade in land had been forbidden. After the middle of the Spring and Autumn Period some of the land gradually passed from the aristocracy to the newly-rising landlord class and to the peasants. During the Warring States Period which followed, the sale and purchase of land became a common occurrence. The newly-rising class of landowners obtained large tracts of land from the princes and their ministers and leased the land to the tillers, collecting rent in the form of a fixed amount of agricultural produce. In this way payment-in-kind gradually replaced the payment of land rent by labour service (corvée). As a result of this modification in the form of land rent, the landowner's control of the tiller's person was considerably weakened.

3. The rise in the level of the productive forces led to a general development of local economy in addition to

changes in the system of landownership. Under Western Zhou, the Wei River valley had been economically the most developed area. In the Spring and Autumn Period, however, the whole Huanghe River valley was transformed into a flourishing region. The economies of the vassal states of Qi (in Shandong), Jin (in Shanxi), Zheng (in central Henan), Song (in eastern Henan), Qin (in Shaanxi) and Chu (in Hubei) all advanced. In the closing years of the Spring and Autumn Period when the states of Wu (in Jiangsu) and Yue (in Zhejiang) were fighting for hegemony, the lower reaches of the Changjiang River were brought into the economic system of the Zhou Dynasty. The development of local economy can be verified by a study of ancient relics and remains. Most of the Western Zhou bronzes which have been unearthed belonged to the Zhou royal house and its officials. Practically no cultural relics of the principalities of this period have been found. In contrast, most of the bronzes of the Eastern Zhou period came from the principalities, an indication that the culture and institutions of the principalities gradually became more advanced during the Spring and Autumn Period.

After the middle of the Warring States Period, the domain of the state of Chu embraced the area now covered by the provinces of Hubei, Hunan, Anhui, Jiangsu and Zhejiang and parts of Shandong, Henan, Sichuan and Guizhou. This state contributed a great deal to the development of the southern part of China. Some idea of the brilliance of Chu culture may be gained from the vast number of the Chu period articles which have been excavated during recent years in Anhui, Hunan, Hubei and southern Henan. Among the finds are bamboo and wooden strips with characters incised on them.

The states of Qin, Zhao (in Hebei) and Yan (in Hebei and the Liaodong Peninsula) also extended their territorial limits beyond their former frontiers, and Chu's influence reached out as far as Yunnan. History records that General Zhuang Qiao of Chu led an expedition into Yunnan and established the Kingdom of Dian there, introducing inland culture into that region for the first time.

4. The development of local economy during the Spring and Autumn and Warring States Periods brought with it marked changes in the political structure. Under Western Zhou numerous vassal states were scattered over the Huanghe River valley. When the Spring and Autumn Period was ushered in, the more powerful princes had already extended their domains by military force and had compelled the smaller and weaker states to submit to their will. The five powerful states of Qi, Song, Jin, Qin and Chu were now contending with one another for hegemony. During the transition from the Spring and Autumn to the Warring States Period, the powerful state of Jin was split into the three states of Han (in Henan), Zhao and Wei (in Hebei and Shanxi). These, together with Qi, Qin, Chu and Yan, became seven powerful states in rivalry with each other for conquest and annexation. In short, the general trend in the Spring and Autumn and Warring States Periods was from division to unification. The newly-rising classes of landlords and peasants demanded an end to the separatist rule of the nobles and the establishment of a unified political power. The system of fiefs was partially abolished and superseded by a system of prefectures and counties. Under this new sys-

tem prefectural governors and county magistrates were appointed by the king and were directly responsible to him. The practice of rewarding a person with a fief, a feudal estate, gradually yielded to a system of payment-in-kind.

The Culture of the Spring and Autumn and Warring States Periods By the end of the Spring and Autumn Period, classical learning was coming into flower. Confucius (552-479 B.C.), champion of the feudal hierarchy, played a very important role in summarizing and spreading academic knowledge. The social and economic upheavals of the Warring States Period made a profound impact on the realm of ideas and led to theoretical controversies in which a "hundred schools of thought" contended with one another to make their voices heard. The Confucians, defending the social hierarchy dominated by the nobles of the time, "modelled themselves upon the traditions of King Wen and King Wu" (i.e., they took Western Zhou as the pattern), and propounded hierarchical and patriarchal principles.

The school of the philosopher Mo Di (480?-390? B.C.) opposed the internecine wars of the princes and the extravagance of the time. The Mohists also indicted the strong for oppressing the weak, the rich for browbeating the poor, the aristocrat for despising the plebeian and the crafty for imposing on the simple-minded. They advocated peace, thrift, brotherhood and mutual help, and reflected the ideology of the oppressed (though not yet rebellious) peasants and petty artisans and traders.

The followers of Lao Zi and Zhuang Zi (365?-290? B.C.) were opposed to social evolution and advocated a return to primitive society in which people lived in isolation all their lives. This school of thought reflected the ideology of the declining aristocracy.

The legalists, represented by Shang Yang (390?-338 B.C.) and Han Fei (280?-233 B.C.), advocated a centralized monarchy and rule by law. They were formulating the political demands of the newly-rising landlord class.

These rival schools of philosophy reflected the contradictions then existing between the different classes and threw light on their conflicting interests.

There was great progress in natural sciences during this period. Chinese astronomers were already familiar with the principal constellations and could calculate the movement of the sun, the moon and the five planets, Mercury, Venus, Mars, Jupiter and Saturn. Hydraulic engineers like Li Bing and Zheng Guo accomplished a great deal in the building of irrigation and water conservancy works. Geographers came to realize, through the development of communications, that China did not constitute the whole world and began to interest themselves in the geography of other lands. Progress was also made in physics, and in the works of Mo Di there is reference to some of the elementary principles of light and mechanics.

A number of historical works appeared. The *Commentary on Confucius' Spring and Autumn Annals by Zuo Qiuming, The Discourses on the States, The Records of the Warring States* and the *Annals of the Bamboo Books* were all written during the Warring States Period. In literature even more important developments were recorded, and long theoretical essays made their appearance in addition to narrative compositions. The long lyrical poems of the Chu poet of genius, Qu Yuan (c. 340-c. 278 B.C.), and the works of other Chu poets, known under the general name of *The Ballads of Chu,* like the *Book of Songs*, constitute a particularly valuable part of China's literary heritage.

II. QIN, HAN, THE THREE KINGDOMS, JIN AND THE SOUTHERN AND NORTHERN DYNASTIES (3rd Century B.C.-6th Century A.D.)

The Qin Dynasty (221-206 B.C.) Shi Huang Di (246-210 B.C.), First Emperor of the Qin Dynasty, conquered the six states of Han, Zhao, Wei, Chu, Yan and Qi. He put an end to the independent, disunited feudal states which had existed for over eight hundred years and founded the first centralized, autocratic feudal empire in Chinese history in 221 B.C.

The appearance of this large empire was a historic victory for the new landlord class. During the Warring States Period this class had obtained the right to own land and had gradually secured control of the principal branches of the social economy. It now demanded an end to the division of the country by the nobles and sought to establish a centralized government under its own domination.

Emperor Shi Huang Di adopted a new system of prefectures and counties to replace the old system of feudal fiefs. He repealed the system of private ownership of land by the nobles and replaced it by one of free trade in land. His contributions towards unifying the country and removing local differences and peculiarities include standardization of weights and measures, the length of the axles of carts, the type of dress and the calendar and the initiation of a single currency, nationally enforced laws, and a unitary script. All the walls, fortifications and barriers between the former states were demolished. Xianyang (now a city bearing the same name in Shaanxi), the capital, became the metropolitan centre, and a network of broad highways linked the whole country. Water-borne traffic extended as far as present-day Guangdong Province. Many large commercial cities came into being, the improved communication system enabling merchants and traders to travel freely between them.

In order to consolidate his new regime, Shi Huang Di had all the arms and weapons held by the people collected and destroyed. He banished some of the former nobles and wealthy gentry of the six conquered states to frontier regions, and forced others to reside in the capital, Xianyang. He sought to stamp out the old aristocratic culture and ideas. In 213 B.C. there was a public burning of books in which an enormous number of books were consigned to the flames, only books on medicine, pharmacy, astronomy and agronomy were exempt from this wanton destruction. Scholars and students who were hostile to the new regime and who denounced the present and praised the past were buried alive in groups.

Shi Huang Di and his successor, the Second Emperor (reigned 209-207 B.C.), both exploited the labour power of the people without scruples. They collected as much as two-thirds of the harvested crops as land rent and, as a result, large tracts of land belonging to the peasants fell into the hands of the landlords and merchants. They forced 300,000 men to build the Great Wall and dispatched 500,000 to garrison Lingnan (Guangdong). An additional 700,000 men were used to build palaces, an equal number to erect Shi Huang Di's mausoleum, and myriads more were conscripted to build roads. As a result, taxation and enforced labour service became so onerous that the peasants had no time to till their own fields and their womenfolk had no time for spinning or weaving. It was literally impossible for the peasants to exist under such burdens. The inevitable happened. In 209 B.C. peasants led by Chen Sheng (?-208 B.C.) and Wu Guang (?-208 B.C.) rose in revolt. Armed only with hoes and clubs, they destroyed the rule of the Qin Dynasty.

The Establishment of the Western Han Dynasty (206 B.C.-24 A.D.) and Its Development In 206 B.C. Liu Bang (256-195 B.C.), one of the peasant leaders later known as Emperor Gao Di of Han, established sovereignty over the whole of China and founded the powerful Han Dynasty, making Changan (now Xian) its capital. In history it became known as Western Han.

The establishment of Western Han was the fruit of a peasant uprising. The history of China demonstrates that a peasant uprising can overthrow an old ruler, but cannot abolish the feudal system. The successful leaders of peasant uprisings inevitably become landlords, and in turn oppress the peasants. The institutions of Western Han were patterned on those of Qin, and their purpose was to safeguard the property and political power of the landlord class and keep the peasants in subjection. The power of the peasants, manifested in the uprisings, compelled the new rulers to make some political and economic concessions to them. These concessions were also favourable to the development of the social economy in the interests of the new rulers who could not establish a powerful and prosperous dynasty without a developed economy.

In order to revive the rural economy, the Western Han administration adopted some repressive measures against merchants who manipulated market prices and indulged in speculative dealings. Merchants were debarred from holding office. In consequence they entered into collusion with the local princedoms and assisted local separatist forces to defy the central government.

During the half century from the reign of Hui Di to that of Jing Di (194-141 B.C.), the local separatist elements and the centralized authority were constantly in conflict. Jing Di succeeded in putting down the rebellion of seven princedoms and further consolidated the unity of the country. Under Wu Di (reigned 140-87 B.C.) the Western Han reached the zenith of its power and the central government wielded unlimited authority. Confucianism, which reflected the concept of centralized power, held sway, and rival schools of thought were opposed. The Five Classics taught by Confucian scholars were used as the standard texts in the royal academy, and Confucianism became the orthodox Chinese doctrine.

During the early years of the Western Han Dynasty, rural economy began to recover from the effects of previous wars. By the time of the reign of Wu Di, the further consolidation of central government power and the mitigation of the local character of the social economy brought greater prosperity to the landlords and merchants. In the course of this development, however, concentration of land assumed increasingly dangerous proportions.

Industry, still in the handicraft stage, extended and merchants amassed large fortunes by smelting iron and producing salt. Some merchant families employed as many as one thousand people. The iron works in Changan and some in the prefectures were most important government enterprises. The Gold and Silver Workshop in

Sichuan, the East and West Weaving Mills at Changan, and the "Factories for Making Fabrics for Three Seasons" at Qi, were all big government establishments, hundreds of millions of cash being invested in them. Bronze casting, lacquer, wood and bamboo work, embroidery, dyeing, and distilling were all on a higher level than during the preceding dynasties, both from the point of view of technical skill and quantity of output.

The development of handicrafts gave an impetus to commercial activity. Changan was the main centre of trade, and Luoyang (in present-day Henan), Chengdu (in Sichuan), Handan (in Hebei), Linzi (in Shandong) and Nanyang (in Henan) all became busy and prosperous commercial cities. The bigger merchants in the cities and towns engaged in speculation and usury, the lesser ones became their own masters and opened shops, buying cheap and selling dear. The economy of different regions became more closely integrated, as innumerable vehicles and boats transported merchandise from one part of the country to another.

Amid an all-round development of the social economy, close economic and cultural ties grew among the different ethnic groups in the country. During Wu Di's reign Western Han established prefectures in present-day Guangdong and Fujian and in the southwest regions, strengthening its control over these areas. In the north and northwest it waged protracted, large-scale wars against Xiong Nu, who had long harassed its borders.

The wars against Xiong Nu lasted ninety years, from the beginning of the reign of Wu Di (140 B.C.) to the end of Xuan Di's reign (73-49 B.C.). Under the command of two renowned generals, Wei Qing (?-106 B.C.) and Huo Qubing (?-117 B.C.), Western Han armies won decisive victories. In 51 B.C. Xiong Nu surrendered, became vassals of the Western Han, and ceased to be a serious threat in the north.

The story started with the various small states which Xiong Nu had taken in the Western Regions (a general reference in the Han period to areas beyond present-day Yumenguan Pass in Gansu Province). In 138 B.C. Wu Di sent Zhang Qian (?-114 B.C.) to these regions. Zhang Qian discovered that there were many wealthy and prosperous countries in the distant West. In 121 B.C. Western Han troops opened a route through the Gansu Corridor to the Western Regions. Later, with the co-operation of the Wu Sun people, Western Han troops smashed the rule of Xiong Nu north and south of the Tianshan Mountains, and converted the various petty states of the Western Regions into vassal states of Western Han. From that time on, traders from China and central Asia sent Chinese merchandise, particularly silks, to the Far West: Da Yuan, Kang Ju, Da Xia, Persia, India, and to the key cities of the Roman Empire. From those countries they brought back products needed by Western Han rulers and the people in the central plains. Western Han reached the height of its power with its conquest of Xiong Nu and the opening up of the Western Regions.

Land Concentration Under Western Han and Peasant Uprisings The half century after Yuan Di's reign (48-33 B.C.) was a period of decline and decay for Western Han. There was corruption at the court, and relatives of the women members of the imperial family[1] and favourite ministers of the sovereigns became important political personages. They amassed enormous fortunes through

---

[1] Mother, wife and favourite concubines of the emperor.

embezzlement, extortion, theft, bribery and other abuses of court privileges.

During and after the reign of Wu Di taxes became more numerous and burdensome. The emperor's annual income from the land, poll, military service, hay, business and property taxes and from the salt and iron monopolies established by Wu Di amounted to thousands of millions of cash. Every peasant was forced to perform up to ninety days of unpaid labour service each year in addition to the payment of taxes. Such ruthless exploitation deprived the peasant of almost all the results of his toil.

Around 50 B.C. the problem of landownership, which had long required solution, became very acute, and the Western Han government was compelled to rent out uncultivated land, and even government land in the neighbourhood of the imperial parks to be cultivated by the peasants. Political oppression, coupled with the exploitation of the peasantry by means of usurious loans, further undermined rural economy. At the same time estates of the officials and landlords each occupying tens of thousands of mu[1] of land existed everywhere in the country. On one occasion, the emperor made a grant of 200,000 mu to a favourite minister.

According to a census taken in the year 2 A.D., the total population of China at the time was sixty million while 800 million mu of land was under cultivation. The relentless exploitation of the peasants drove many of them from their land and made them homeless. Some were herded together and sold with cattle, others had no

---

[1] Weights and measures vary in different areas and at different periods in Chinese history. According to the standards today, a mu is 0.0666 of a hectare, or 0.1647 of an acre. — *Translator.*

alternative but to sell themselves into slavery. The number of official retainers in the service of the rich exceeded 100,000. They did no productive work, and their upkeep was a heavy burden on the peasants. The situation in the countryside deteriorated to such an extent that it was regarded as a privilege to be a slave, as starvation was the common lot of the peasant grain-producers. Meanwhile the emperor and the rich and powerful fed their horses on the grain denied to the peasants.

About 30 B.C. a long series of natural calamities, including floods and droughts, struck the countryside over wide areas. This led to uprisings of peasants and handicraftsmen. The uprisings were suppressed, but the social crisis deepened. During one year of severe famine in the district around Changan, a catty of gold (worth about 10,000 cash) was bartered for five *sheng*[1] of beans. People were driven desperate by starvation.

In an attempt to ease the ever-sharpening social contradictions and save the threatened rule of the landlord class, Wang Mang (?-23 A.D.), a relative of a woman member of the imperial family, who had usurped the throne, introduced a programme of reforms in the year 9 A.D. Its principal features were: (1) ownership of all land by the emperor and prohibition of the private sale and purchase of land; (2) prohibition of trade in private slaves; (3) the appointment in Changan and five other principal cities (Luoyang, Handan, Linzi, Nanyang and Chendu) of officials whose function was to control prices and extend low-interest loans to peasants; and (4) government administration of salt, iron, wine and three other commodities to prevent speculation in them by the

[1] A *sheng* is about 0.028 of a bushel.

merchants; and (5) currency reform. The object of Wang Mang's reforms was to put some pressure on the landlords and merchants and to lessen the prevailing social tension.

Wang Mang relied upon the landlords and merchants, however, to enforce these reforms, with the result that they were frequently revised. The peasants consequently suffered heavy losses, and their plight became desperate. In 22 A.D. a series of uprisings, led by groups known as Xinshi, Pinglin, Red Eyebrows and Bronze-Horses, took place in the basins of the Changjiang and Huanghe rivers. The peasant armies succeeded in breaking into the capital city and the government of Wang Mang was overthrown.

The Rise of Eastern Han (25-220 A.D.) and Its Development While the flames of peasant wars were raging Liu Xiu (5 B.C.-57 A.D.), son of a landlord of the Han house, assembled a strong force in Nanyang, Henan Province. He suppressed the peasant insurgent armies and eliminated many local leaders who had taken advantage of the general confusion to set up independent regimes. In 25 A.D. he established his capital at Luoyang and restored the Han Dynasty. Chinese historians call this dynasty the Eastern Han Dynasty.

Liu Xiu, who became known as Emperor Guang Wu Di, was determined to collect the land tax in full and ordered a new survey of all the land in the country. He also decreed that all slaves should be emancipated so that former peasants who had been divorced from production could return to farming. These orders were not fully carried out because of opposition by the landlord class, but the peasant rebellions forced the landlords to make some concessions. As a result, the social economy began to improve during and after the reign of Ming Di (reigned 58-75), and many abandoned water conservancy works were restored. For example, at Runan (in present-day Henan) where a system of ponds served as water reservoirs extending for 200 kilometres, the cost of repair amounted to thirty million cash in one year. The Changjiang valley became more developed and, in general, agriculture became as prosperous as under Western Han.

The technique of the handicrafts improved, and water-power began to be used to drive the bellows for iron smelting and casting. Crafts which had come into existence during the Western Han period were further developed. The output of the preceding dynasty was outstripped, mainly because of a greater division of labour. Judging from the inscriptions of some lacquer cups unearthed at Lak Lang in Korea, these utensils passed through the hands of many artisans during the course of production.

There were many inventions during this period, the most important being the making of paper in the year 105 by Cai Lun. The manufacture of porcelain also commenced during the Eastern Han Dynasty.

The cities became more prosperous. Luoyang replaced Changan as the political and commercial centre of the country. Western Han cities continued to develop under the new regime, and Panyu (Guangzhou) and Xuwen in Guangdong became coastal ports for foreign trade.

In the opening years of the Eastern Han Dynasty Xiong Nu split into two groups, the Northern and the Southern. Each was determined to destroy the other. The Southern Xiong Nu joined with Eastern Han to attack the northern group. In the year 73 A.D. the troops of Eastern Han defeated the Northern Xiong Nu and reopened the road leading to the Western Regions. After repeated attacks by Xianbei in the east and by the

Eastern Han Dynasty in the south, the Northern Xiong Nu fell apart in the next ten years and more. Some surrendered to Eastern Han, others submitted to the authority of Xianbei, and the rest was forced to migrate further west.

Acting in co-ordination with the advance of its expeditionary forces, the Eastern Han government sent an official, Ban Chao (34-102), on a political mission to the Western Regions. His arrival there marked the re-entry of these regions into the historical scene. The prestige of the dynasty enabled Ban Chao to establish the rule of Eastern Han over them, and Chinese traders again carried silk and iron to the Western world. In 97 Ban Chao dispatched an emissary, Gan Ying, to establish contact with Da Qin (Rome). Gan Ying succeeded in getting as far as the Persian Gulf.

Internal Struggles of the Ruling Class, the Uprising of the Yellow Turbans and the Disintegration of Eastern Han Large numbers of men were drafted into the army or compelled to render labour service to carry on the wars against Xiong Nu. This reduced the peasantry to the verge of bankruptcy. The wars brought in large quantities of booty, but the enormous wealth which was thus seized or made by barter did not go to the peasants. It flowed into the hands of a few nobles, officials, landlords and merchants, who used it to dispossess the peasants of their holdings.

The destruction of the rural economy weakened Eastern Han's power to control its vassal states. It is, therefore, not surprising that towards the beginning of the second century the various small states and tribes in the west, which had been conquered by Eastern Han, began to throw off the yoke of oppression. The Qiang tribesmen, a nomadic people living on the steppes of Gansu and Qinghai, were the first to revolt. They blocked the Gansu Corridor leading to the Western Regions, bringing the Eastern Han Dynasty under an imminent threat. The struggle between Eastern Han and the Qiang tribesmen lasted for nearly forty years, and although the latter were eventually subdued, an enormous military bill had to be defrayed, with the result that the people were further exhausted and impoverished. Eastern Han never recovered from the effects of this campaign. A number of other wars of this character accentuated the economic crisis and sharpened political contradictions. The dynasty was rapidly tottering to a fall.

From the end of the first century cliques had been formed among relatives of the women members of the imperial family and the court eunuchs, each trying to destroy the other in their scrambles for the control of the government. They practised open bribery and embezzlement and perverted justice. They exploited the poor and extorted huge sums of money from the rich members of the other political camps. They not only stole from the national treasury but also robbed travellers. They excluded many men of ability and talent from official positions. All this led to the sharpening of the struggles within the ruling class.

Nobles and officials, particularly officials of lower rank and students of the imperial academy, were oppressed by the eunuchs. They banded together and formed a political association to oppose their common enemy. The students "criticized the high officials and ministers of the government". They mobilized public opinion against the eunuchs, and organized student demonstrations, thousands strong, which went to the imperial palace and submitted memorials requesting that the eunuchs be put under control. These struggles were shortlived, for the eunuchs took violent repressive measures. Hundreds of people were killed and thousands were thrown into prison.

While these internal struggles were going on within the ranks of the propertied class, there was a daily intensifying conflict between the antagonistic classes. Peasant riots frequently occurred, culminating in the year 184 in the nation-wide uprising of the Yellow Turbans led by Zhang Jiao (?-184). Although this uprising was eventually crushed by the troops of the landlord class, the remnants of the Yellow Turbans, together with other peasant armed units which had risen against the central authority, maintained armed resistance against the landlords, hastening the disintegration of Eastern Han.

The Cultural Achievements of Western and Eastern Han

Under Western and Eastern Han culture made marked progress. In the realm of historical writing, the *Historical Records* by Sima Qian (148 B.C.-?) introduced a new form of biography, and the *History of Han* by Ban Gu (32-92) inaugurated the method of recording history by dynasties. Both methods set the style for the writing of dynastic histories for the following two thousand years. In the field of literature writers of genius like Sima Xiangru (180-118 B.C.) and Zhang Heng (78-139) appeared. In philosophy, the materialist Wang Chong (27-?) boldly criticized and denounced the superstitious ideas then advocated at the court. Stone sculptures of human figures, carvings on tomb-stones and paintings on lacquer during the Han Dynasty were important contributions to Chinese art. Zhang Heng, as a scientist, invented an armillary sphere operated by water power, a seismoscope, and an instrument to detect the direction of the wind. The polar properties of the magnet were also discovered in the early years of Eastern Han. These inventions and discoveries were linked with progress made in the science of astronomy and the arrangement of the calendar during Western and Eastern Han.

From the Three Kingdoms to the Unification Under Western Jin The landlords organized their own armed forces at the time of the great uprising of the Yellow Turbans. These armed bands co-operated in the massacre of the peasants, but they also frequently engaged in internecine warfare. Finally three leaders survived. Cao Cao (155-220) occupied the Huanghe River valley and set up the Kingdom of Wei (220-265) with capital at Luoyang; Liu Bei (161-223) occupied Sichuan and set up the Kingdom of Shu (221-263) with capital at Chengdu; and Sun Quan (182-252) occupied the middle and lower reaches of the Changjiang River and set up the Kingdom of Wu (222-280) with capital at Nanjing. This was known as the Three Kingdoms Period which began in 220 and ended in 280 when Western Jin conquered the Kingdom of Wu.

As a result of the continual warfare between various warlords in the closing years of Eastern Han, the Huanghe River valley, the cradle of Chinese economy and civilization, suffered appalling devastation. The once populous rural communities now disappeared, and the once busy, prosperous cities and towns were reduced to mounds of rubble. Thousands of peasants were slaughtered or died of hunger, disease and pestilence. The population was much lower than during the Western and Eastern Han dynasties.

Despite incessant warfare, the rural economy under

the Three Kingdoms gradually recovered. The rulers of these states, the state of Wei in particular, ensured an adequate supply of grain for the armed forces by instituting a system of military colonies, under which the garrison troops were made to cultivate land and grow crops. Because of the same military requirements, war industry, still in the handicraft stage, was specially developed. For example, Zhuge Liang (181-234), a renowned prime minister and strategist of the state of Shu, invented a bow which could shoot ten arrows simultaneously. He also devised a light vehicle for carrying grain known as "wooden oxen and running horses". Ma Jun, who lived in the Kingdom of Wei, constructed and improved an artillery wagon which could project stone balls. Sun Quan, the Wu ruler, built big ships and organized a fleet manned by 10,000 men to sail to the South Sea Islands and the Liaodong Peninsula. The weaving loom improved by Ma Jun came into use in the north. In Sichuan natural gas was used for boiling brine to produce salt. These successes speeded up the economic recovery of the country. In literature, poems and prose-poems reached new levels of development. Cao Cao and his son Cao Zhi (192-232) and the seven outstanding scholars (Kong Rong, Chen Lin, Wang Can, Xu Gan, Ruan Yu, Ying Yang, and Liu Zhen) of the Jian'an period (196-220) were all literary giants. The teachings of Confucius still held the leading position in the world of thought, but there was also a great interest in the study of metaphysical naturalism. The latter reflected the tendency of the landlord class towards escapism.

With the recovery of the social economy, and particularly with the comparatively rapid development in the Huanghe River valley, a section of the landlord class, headed by the Sima family, began to struggle for the establishment of unified political power. The Simas overthrew the Kingdoms of Shu and Wei and founded the Jin Dynasty (265-316). Finally, in 280, the Kingdom of Wu was also vanquished, and the disunion that had existed under the Three Kingdoms was now ended and a unified state re-established.

In the same year when Sima Yan, known as the Emperor Wu Di of Jin (236-290), conquered Wu, the Land Allocation System was introduced. This provided for the allocation of a definite amount of land to peasants, its primary purpose being to resettle those who had lost their holdings. Peasants were now forced to till their land, pay a fixed amount of tax for it and carry out various forms of labour service.

Through the introduction of the Land Allocation System, however, the majority of the peasantry did receive some land. This had a stabilizing effect on the country, and people were described as being happy and content in the decade 280-290. Nevertheless, the powerful and the mighty were indulging in the practice of land appropriation, thus undermining the Land Allocation System. The ruling class, with Wu Di as its acknowledged leader, was accustomed to a wasteful and degenerate mode of life and lived riotously on the enormous wealth squeezed from the peasantry. History records that the "extravagance of the period cost more than natural calamities".

The unification achieved by Jin was soon shattered. After the death of Wu Di, relentless struggles for power broke out between the nobles. These struggles are historically known as the "Disturbances of the Eight Princes". In the eighteen years of uninterrupted internecine wars that followed, the areas on the lower reaches of the Huanghe River were drenched in blood. These wars wore out the Jin Dynasty and weakened its defensive strength.

The Sixteen States The years between 304 and 439 were years in which the northern part of China suffered great destruction. Xiong Nu overthrew Jin and thereafter various tribes — Jie, Xian Bei, Di and Qiang — successively occupied the central part of China, while other tribes seized frontier areas. They established shortlived kingdoms. This period is known in Chinese history as that of the Sixteen States. It was not until Northern Wei unified the northern part of China in 386 that the intertribal wars came to an end.

The nomads living beyond the northern and northwestern frontiers had been moving towards the interior ever since the time of Eastern Han. This movement continued unabated throughout the period of the Three Kingdoms and Jin. The ruling class of Jin ruthlessly exploited and oppressed these settlers, treating them far more cruelly than they did the local-born peasants. The nomads were comprised of the following tribes:

Xiong Nu, who had migrated into the Fenhe River valley (in present-day Shanxi Province), had been reduced to tragic straits under the Han Dynasty, the Kingdom of Wei and particularly during the Jin period. The majority of them were tenants of the landlords of Han nationality;[1] some were seized by Han rulers and sold

---

[1] The term Han nationality (or the Han people or the Han) embraces the majority of the inhabitants of China other than those of the ethnic minorities. It is taken from *Han* of the Han Dynasty when the Chinese people were known as Han beyond the borders. — *Translator.*

into slavery. This eventually led, during the closing years of the Jin Dynasty, to an uprising of the Xiong Nu people under their leader Liu Yuan (?-310). They took Luoyang and Changan, captured two Jin emperors, Huai Di and Ming Di, and destroyed the rule of Jin in the Huanghe River valley. They founded the Kingdom of Han which was subsequently renamed Zhao, historically known as the Former Zhao, to be distinguished from its conqueror Later Zhao.

The Jie tribe followed the example of Xiong Nu and rose against Jin rule. Some members of this tribe had settled in Shanxi and many of them were treated by Jin rulers as slaves, being bought and sold like chattels. During the uprising of Xiong Nu, Shi Le (?-333), a Jie, who had once been sold into slavery, rallied his tribesmen and many outcasts among the Han people in Henan in a struggle against Jin. Shi Le's forces grew in power and established the state of Later Zhao, which attacked and vanquished Former Zhao and occupied the main part of northern China.

After controlling the Liaohe River valley in the northeast, the Xian Bei people covered the whole of northern China except Gansu which was held by a Han, Zhang Gui (255-314). He founded Former Liang, which was conquered by the Di people.

The year 351 saw the rise of the Di tribesmen in Shaanxi. They founded Former Qin. Under the ruler Fu Jian (338-385), the tribesmen overthrew Former Yan which had been established by the Xian Bei people as well as Former Liang established by Zhang Gui. Thus they re-unified the north. In 383 Fu Jian proceeded southward on a large-scale invasion of Eastern Jin. His army was routed in the Feishui River valley, and the defeat was soon followed by the fall of Former Qin.

During the next half century there was continuous warfare and numerous shortlived kingdoms appeared in the north and then vanished. Countless people were killed, cattle carried away and productive forces scattered and destroyed. Cities and towns were sacked and devastated, large tracts of land were laid waste.

During this period the majority of the Han nobles, officials, landlords and merchants fled to the Changjiang River valley. The Han people who remained in the north united for a time in armed self-defence, made use of natural barriers, dug entrenchments and built barracks and ramparts. Under the increasing pressure of the ethnic minorities their resistance was mostly crushed. The landlords went over to the invaders and helped them persecute Han peasants. Thus the peasants led an extremely miserable life under the double oppression of the landlords and the invaders, and the economy and culture in the northern part of China suffered disastrous losses.

Eastern Jin; the Southern Dynasties When the northern part of China was divided into a number of states, Emperor Yuan Di of Eastern Jin (317-420), with the support of the big southern landlords, established in 317 a dynasty dominated by the Han nationality in the Changjiang River basin. It was followed by four successive dynasties under Han rulers: Song (420-479), Qi (479-502), Liang (502-557) and Chen (557-589). They became known as the Southern Dynasties. The political power of Eastern Jin was composed of the big immigrant families of aristocratic landlords from the north and received support from the big landlords south of Changjiang. The northern aristocratic landlords, claiming the sole right to enter the civil service, consolidated their political power and prevented the southern big landlords from holding high office. They exercised special discrimination against the scholars of humble origin (common landlords), forbidding friendship and intermarriage with them. As a result, a sharp clash of interests developed between the northern and the southern landlords, and there was prolonged internal dissension in the ranks of the ruling class. Under the rule of Song and Qi, some people of humble origin were allowed to participate in the high councils of the government. Although this implied recognition of political equality, their social standing remained low, and they were still despised by the aristocratic families.

Some of the refugees from the north settled in districts south of the Huaihe River or in northern Jiangsu and reclaimed land there. Others became tenant-farmers or slaves of the southern aristocratic landlords, the greater part of the land in the region south of Changjiang having already been appropriated by the big southern landlords. The refugee nobles from the north obtained land by purchase or by imperial grant. They also proceeded to cultivate wasteland and forcibly occupied mountainous and swampy regions. The peasants had only very small plots of land and had to bear a heavy burden of taxation in addition to having to provide labour service. This state of affairs led to two peasant uprisings, one in 399 led by Sun En (?-402) and the other by Tang Yuzhi in 485.

The refugees who went south took with them the advanced agricultural technique of the central part of the country and played an important role in developing the south. The resulting advance in agriculture, coupled with the introduction of the tea shrub, and the production of porcelain, created favourable conditions for the growth of handicrafts and the development of trade. The urban economy south of Changjiang showed marked progress from Eastern Jin to the Chen Dynasty. The ruling class made use of their special privileges while conducting trade, and many commercial cities rose on the banks of the Changjiang River. Trading and municipal taxes and customs duties became important sources of government revenue. During the three hundred years of Wu, Eastern Jin and the Southern Dynasties, the economic development of the Changjiang valley reached a position second only to that of the central regions.

Because of the southward migration of many scholarly families, Jiankang (modern Nanjing) became the political centre of the Southern Dynasties and the cultural centre of China during the fourth, fifth and sixth centuries. Poets, painters and scholars gathered there, and literature and art flourished. A number of scientific discoveries were made and the mathematician Zu Chongzhi (429-500) made a remarkable calculation, namely, the ratio of the circumference to the diameter of a circle was between 3.1415926 and 3.1415927.

The Northern Dynasties During the period of great divisions in the north, Toba, a branch of the Xian Bei tribe, rose in what is now the northern part of Shanxi Province. When Toba came into contact with Han culture, their society changed from one of primitive communism to slavery and then from slavery to feudalism. By the aid of their powerful cavalry, after considerable fighting, they brought the north under unified control and established the Northern Wei Dynasty (386-534) with Pingcheng (modern Datong) as capital.

The rule of Northern Wei brought no less sufferings to the common people than that of the Sixteen States it replaced. In 485 Emperor Xiao Wen Di (reigned 471-499) introduced a system of land equalization which provided for the allotment of a fixed amount of land to adults, both men and women. The landless peasants were given unclaimed wasteland to cultivate for a specified period. At the same time a census was taken, and the big landlords were deprived of the service of those peasants who had been under their control and who were now required to pay taxes. In order to lessen the big landlords' opposition the new land system recognized their title to the land in their possession and granted additional land to their slaves.

After this system came into operation the acreage of arable land increased and agriculture developed rapidly. A book written at the close of the Northern Wei Dynasty by Jia Sixie, entitled *Important Arts for Educating the People,* gives a detailed description of the methods employed in agriculture and animal husbandry and shows the development of agricultural technique of that time.

Commerce in Northern Wei lagged far behind that in the region south of Changjiang. Barter was widely practised, and metal coins did not come into use until 495.

The Han comprised the great majority of the people ruled by Northern Wei, and in order to keep them in subjection, Northern Wei rulers selected certain Han landlords to join their government.

In order to win the co-operation of Han landlords and

consolidate his rule, Emperor Xiao Wen Di carried out a firm policy of adoption of Han culture. In 494 he moved his capital to Luoyang, where he set up various institutions and passed laws similar to those operating under the Southern Dynasties. He changed the multisyllabic surnames of Xian Bei to the monosyllabic surnames of the Han. He forbade his Xian Bei officials to speak their own language or wear tribal costumes at court, and encouraged the Xian Bei nobles to marry into the big Han landlord families. These measures did bring about a closer relationship between the Xian Bei and the Han landlords, but at the same time their joint oppression provoked Han and Xian Bei peasants to join hands against them.

A powerful tribe known as Rou Ran, inhabiting the Mongolian plateau, constantly harassed the border and threatened Northern Wei territory, and Northern Wei established six garrison posts along the frontier. After the removal of the capital to Luoyang, the political centre of the country shifted southwards. The commanders of the six garrisons, their officers and men then fell out of royal favour, and in 524 they mutinied on a large scale. This was followed by a big uprising of Han and Xian Bei peasants. The peasant uprising failed, but Northern Wei split into Eastern Wei (534-550) and Western Wei (535-557). Later Gao Yang, a Han, overthrew the government of Eastern Wei and established the Northern Qi Dynasty (550-577). Yuwen Jue, a Xian Bei, secured control of the Western Wei government and founded Northern Zhou (557-581). The rulers of Northern Qi were corrupt and brutal and aroused the resentment and hatred of the people. On the other hand, the rulers of Northern Zhou introduced reforms and encouraged production, with the result that their power grew. Northern Zhou eventually conquered Northern Qi, paving the way for the unification of China under the Sui Dynasty.

The Influence of Buddhism on Politics, Economic Life and Culture Buddhism, which was introduced into China through Da Yue Di about the beginning of the Christian era, gradually spread during the Eastern Han Dynasty and the period of the Three Kingdoms. The study of metaphysics was very much in vogue during Wei and Jin, and Buddhism spread among the literati amid their study of metaphysics. Towards the close of Eastern Jin, Buddhism became linked with Confucian ritualism which had dominated feudal society. The Buddhist ideas of transmigration and retribution were widely accepted and the power of the ruling class was further consolidated by this linking of feudal ritualism with Buddhism.

The spread of Buddhism gradually reduced the ranks of the Taoists, and Taoism lost ground in the controversies between the followers of the two beliefs. Controversies also developed between some of the Confucian scholars and the Buddhists. During the reign of Emperor Wu Di (502-549) of the Liang Dynasty, Fan Zhen, a Confucian scholar, proclaimed the theory of the destructibility of the spirit, contending that the spirit is born with the body and that when the body dies, the spirit goes out with it. He opposed the doctrines of both transmigration and retribution. The ruling class of the Southern Dynasties, helpless in face of contemporary problems, needed the teaching of Buddhism for their own spiritual consolation and to keep the masses of people quiescent. Wu Di, who regarded the preaching of Buddhism as his main task, retired to a Buddhist temple and became a novice. During the Liang Dynasty there were in Jiankang alone five hundred Buddhist monasteries accommodating a hundred thousand monks and nuns. The monasteries obtained large tracts of land as alms or by forcible occupation, and also acted as pawn-brokers and money-lenders, exploiting the poor by charging exorbitant rates of interest. Buddhist influence hampered the growth of the social economy in the south.

Buddhism flourished in the north too, thanks to the encouragement of the ruling class. Once in 446 the rulers of Northern Wei tried to suppress Buddhism and its priests in favour of Taoism. Buddhist idols were destroyed, but Buddhism survived and spread more widely. Northern rulers later spent enormous sums of money on the building of temples and the maintenance of monasteries. Records show that there were 1,367 temples and monasteries in Luoyang in 534. There was a total of 30,000 temples and monasteries and more than two million monks in the whole of the north. Under Northern Qi and Northern Zhou conditions were about the same as under Northern Wei, and temples and monasteries appropriated land and enslaved the peasants.

Peasant families who sent offerings of grain to the temples and monasteries were described as Buddhist followers' households. Those who cultivated the land owned by the temples and performed various forms of labour service were called Buddhist households. The temples and monasteries consumed a large share of the wealth of society. Like those in the south they were also big landowners and usurers. It was this state of affairs which led to the confiscation of temple property in 574 by Wu Di of Northern Zhou (reigned 561-578), who also ordered the Buddhist monks to return to secular life.

The arts of sculpture and painting associated with Buddhism made great progress. The Thousand-Buddha Grottoes at Dunhuang which started in the Former Liang Dynasty, the stone caves at Bingling Temple, the Grottoes at Maijishan, the stone grottoes at Yungang and Longmen, all dating back to Northern Wei, are now part of China's historical treasury of art. The introduction of Buddhism also brought with it a new type of music, dance, musical instruments, and architecture. The translation of Buddhist sutras into Chinese enriched the language. Under the influence of Buddhism, the doctrine of Taoism acquired a more comprehensive theoretical system.

The *Annotation to the Book of Waterways,* compiled by Li Daoyuan at this time, was a brilliant contribution to Chinese geography.

III. THE PERIODS OF SUI, TANG, THE FIVE DYNASTIES, SONG AND YUAN (6th to 14th Century)

The Unification of China Under Sui and the Fall of Sui (581-618) In 581 Yang Jian (541-604), a Han, who was serving as prime minister under the Xian Bei rulers of Northern Zhou, seized power and established the Sui Dynasty. He became known as Emperor Wen Di of Sui. He vanquished the Chen Dynasty of the Southern Dynasties in 589 and unified the whole of China which had been torn apart ever since the time of Eastern Jin.

His dynasty retained the land equalization system which had been in force since the Northern Wei regime. It lightened the burden of forced labour and taxes on the peasants. As a result of these measures agricultural production advanced and the population gradually increased. The currency system was improved and standard weights and measures were adopted for use throughout the country. The unification of the north and the south created new markets, and handicrafts and trade thrived.

Soon after his accession, the next emperor, Yang Di (reigned 605-618), embarked on an extensive programme of construction. He pressed two million men into service to rebuild the city of Luoyang and another million to repair and lengthen the Great Wall. With Luoyang as the centre, he set men to work digging the Grand Canal in order to connect Hangzhou in the south with Zhuojun (modern Beijing) in the north. The completion of this canal was a great contribution to the development of Chinese economy and culture.

Disregarding the heavy toll of human life and finance exacted by his building programmes, Yang Di launched expeditions against Tuyuhun, a western tribe, and also against Korea. Large levies of men and grain were enforced to carry out these campaigns. Then followed a series of natural calamities, which further impoverished the country and people. Close on the heels of the launching of the Korean campaign broke out a series of peasant uprisings.

In an attempt to prevent such revolts both Wen Di and Yang Di issued repeated edicts forbidding peasants to possess arms, but despite these edicts peasant uprisings continued throughout the closing years of the reign of Yang Di. Historical records tell of more than a hundred such mass uprisings, led by men like Zhai Rang and Dou Jiande and involving millions of peasants. Within the brief span of thirty years the Sui Dynasty was overthrown.

The Establishment of the Tang Dynasty (618-907) and Its Days of Power Li Yuan (565-635), a Sui official known in history as Emperor Gao Zu of Tang, placed himself at the head of the uprisings. He founded the Tang Dynasty in 618 and made Changan his capital.

The peasant wars during the closing years of the Sui Dynasty dealt a serious blow to the rule of the landlords and gave impetus to the development of the productive forces of society.

The next emperor, Tai Zong (reigned 627-649), was an outstanding sovereign. He rapidly restored the feudal order and won great political and military power.

Between his reign and that of Xuan Zong (reigned 712-756), the majority of peasants received land, irrigation work was developed, and the rural economy again prospered.

The state established many handicraft workshops for the production of brocade, carpet weaving and dyeing. The workshops also produced various metal objects, including coins. These establishments employed regular and seasonal workers, government slaves and wage-labourers. Ship-building and the manufacture of bronze mirrors in Yangzhou, the brocade and salt of Sichuan, the porcelain of Jiangxi and the brasswork of Taiyuan (in Shanxi) were renowned throughout the land. Mining also made great headway. There were fifty-eight silver foundries, ninety-six copper foundries, five iron mines, two tin mines and four lead mines in Anhui, Zhejiang and Jiangxi alone. The handicrafts under Tang were much more advanced than those of the preceding ages.

Trade was facilitated by the institution of a courier service and a system of stagecoaches. The opening of the Grand Canal created specially favourable conditions for the flow of merchandise. Changan, Luoyang, Yangzhou and Guangzhou became big commercial centres, and many other cities and towns owed their prosperity to the growth of trade.

The power of Tang continued to extend, reaching far into the northwest. In the early period, its armies defeated the Eastern Turks and then launched an offensive against the Western Turks. The Tang rulers set up a frontier-governer's residency in areas of today's Xinjiang and along Suiye River in Central Asia, and also sent garrisons to Qiuzi (present-day Kuqa in Xinjiang), Yutian (present-day Hotan), Shule (present-day Kashi Shi) and Suiye. These are steps taken by the Tang Dynasty to strengthen its economic and cultural relations with the Western Regions.

In the early seventh century, the leader of the Tubo people, Songtsan Gambo (?-650), united the scattered tribes on the Tibetan Plateau and established his capital in Lhasa. This was the most prosperous time in Tibetan history, when both social economy and culture showed marked progress. In spite of the military clashes between the Tang Dynasty and Tubo, Princess Wen Cheng (?-680) of the Tang court was sent to Tubo and married Songtsan Gambo in Tai Zong's time. The princess took with her many Tang artisans, books about production techniques, vegetable seeds, handicrafts and medicine. In 710 Princess Jin Cheng was married to Tubo, taking with her another hundred skilled workers and Qiuzi music. After Princess Wen Cheng's arrival in Tubo, the economic and cultural ties between the Han and the Tibetan nationalities grew all the closer.

During this time Chinese traders also entered Central Asia and West Asia. Merchants and religious missionaries from the Arab world and other countries travelled to China, and at one time Changan had between four and five thousand foreign residents. The city became a centre for international trade and cultural intercourse, further enriching the material and cultural life of the Chinese people. Cities and towns grew and flourished along the banks of Changjiang and the seacoast, and there was official supervision of import trade and shipping. The dynasty reached the zenith of its power and prosperity. It was during this period that Chinese culture was introduced into Korea and Japan. The art of paper-making which originated in China was carried from China to Central Asia and, several centuries later, was introduced into Europe by the Arabs. Thus China made a great contribution to the growth of culture in the West.

The Internal Strife of the Ruling Class Class contradictions and the contradictions within the ruling class sharpened during the early period (713-741) of Xuan Zong's reign, but there was no open rupture until war broke out in the ranks of the ruling class in 755. The rebellion of An Lushan and Shi Siming, two generals of nomadic origin, marked the beginning of the decline of the Tang Dynasty. From then on the situation rapidly worsened. Military satraps broke away; there was constant strife between rival bureaucratic factions and against control of politics by court eunuchs.

An Lushan, who commanded a garrison at Youzhou, led a revolt against the throne and occupied the capital, Changan. After his death, one of his subordinate officers,

Shi Siming, succeeded to the command of the rebel army and continued to attack the Tang government. The rebel army slaughtered many Han people. This is known in Chinese history as the An-Shi rebellion.

Although the An-Shi rebellion was eventually crushed by Tang forces, it seriously undermined the economy of the country, especially that in the Huanghe River valley. Changan, Luoyang and numerous other cities, towns and villages were ravaged.

The system of military satraps was originally established for the purpose of consolidating Tang rule, but after the An-Shi rebellion the satraps became virtually independent. They pocketed state taxes, organized private armies and established their hereditary positions. Some of them became completely independent of the central government in Changan.

This government was dominated by court eunuchs who grabbed military power, controlled the movement of the army and dictated the appointment and dismissal of officials. The eunuchs even deposed emperors and selected new ones. Eight of the nine emperors after Xian Zong (reigned 806-820) were hand-picked by eunuchs.

The system of choosing men for government service on the recommendation of nobles, practised under the rule of Wei and Jin, was abolished during the Sui and Tang dynasties; it was replaced by a system of competitive examinations. As a result, many young men who came from ordinary landlord and merchant families were able to enter the government. These new officials often came into conflict with the old nobles and bureaucrats. Officials of different social strata formed rival cliques and cabals, and the struggle for power between them lasted decades.

Great Peasant Uprisings Large numbers of peasants were driven from the land or ruined as a result of the wild scramble among nobles, merchants, officials, landlords and Buddhist temples for land. The burden of autumn and summer taxes, and hundreds of miscellaneous levies and imposts fell heavily on their shoulders. Corrupt local officials also made heavy demands on them. Driven desperate, they rose in armed revolt. In 860 a peasant uprising broke out under the leadership of Qiu Fu (?-860). In the same year a mutiny in the army was organized by Pang Xun (?-869). Both were local revolts, but an uprising on a nation-wide scale was on its way. It began in 874 under the leadership of Wang Xianzhi (?-878), at Changyuan County (in modern Henan). In the following year Huang Chao (?-884) led an uprising in Shandong. The peasant armies broke through the encirclement of the government forces and infiltrated into Henan and Hubei. Wang Xianzhi was killed in action in 878 and Huang Chao succeeded him as leader of the peasant armies. He led them from Shandong into Henan, Anhui and Hubei. From Hubei they crossed Changjiang and advanced into the coastal regions of the southeast, pushing through to Guangdong. From Guangdong they entered Guangxi, passed through Hunan, Hubei, Jiangxi and Jiangsu, again crossed the river, and then entered Anhui and Henan. In 880 the peasant forces captured the capital, Changan, and organized a government with Huang Chao at its head.

After holding Changan for two years and four months, the peasant forces were driven out of the city by the combined pressure of the Tang government and Sha Tuo, a branch of the Western Turks. They were annihilated shortly afterwards.

The collapse of the Tang Dynasty followed.

The Disintegration of the Tang Dynasty and the Rise of the Five Dynasties and Ten States In 907 Zhu Wen overthrew the rule of Tang and founded the Later Liang Dynasty. This was followed in rapid succession by the Later Tang, Later Jin, Later Han and Later Zhou dynasties, all of which occupied the basin of the Huanghe River. They became known in Chinese history as the Five Dynasties (907-960).

In the same period, there were also ten independent feudal states in other parts of the country, known as the Ten States. China was again plunged into a period of disunity.

About this time the State of Khitan (916-1125) rose in the Liaohe River valley in the northeast. They occupied sixteen prefectures (in Shanxi and the northern part of Hebei) and changed the title of their state to Liao. Liao made Yanjing (Beijing) its capital and gradually became very powerful.

Following the fall of the Tang Dynasty, the economy of the country suffered seriously as a result of the ravages of war. According to historical records, by the time of the Five Dynasties, the people near Changan "fled to the mountain fastnesses, leaving their fields uncultivated for years on end". Some of the cities were reduced to ruins. In the city of Changan only a few of the palaces, monasteries, government buildings and civilian houses survived the fires of war. In Luoyang, as one historical record puts it, "the ground was strewn with human bones, while brambles and thorn bushes grew everywhere. There were less than a hundred households left". It was also recorded that from Hangu Pass in the west to Shandong in the east, and from Henan in the north to the Changjiang and Huai river valleys in the south, "birds scattered and fish could hardly survive, human settlements were few, and desolation reigned supreme".

The rulers of the various states tried to restore economic order in their respective domains, but as they enlarged their armed forces for the consolidation of their power, they bled the people white, imposing exorbitant taxes and levies and innumerable forms of forced labour on the peasantry. This only aggravated the poverty and misery in the countryside.

Because of the split-up and disunity in the country during the period of the Five Dynasties and the Ten States, many cities became political centres, especially those in the south such as Chengdu, Jinling (Nanjing), Fuzhou, Hangzhou, Guangzhou, Jingzhou and Changsha. The rulers of the various feudal states were ruthless in their exploitation of the rural areas and concentrated all their wealth in the cities, which also became the centres of handicraft and commerce.

Literature, Art and Religion in the Tang Dynasty Poetry held the dominant place in Tang's literature. Chinese poetry dates back to early antiquity, and it came to the flower of its glory at this period. The dynasty produced many brilliant poets, like Li Bai (701-762), Du Fu (712-770) and Bai Juyi (772-846). These three rank as the greatest of them. Fifty thousand Tang poems are still extant. Li Bai was a poet of universal genius, whose work "runs like an unbridled steed". Du Fu was a realist whose poems, dignified yet full of warm feeling, portray with superb delicacy the condition of Tang society, especially the sufferings of the peasants, both before and after the rebellion of An Lushan and Shi Siming. Bai

Juyi, who wrote in a popular style, did not lack courage in exposing the dark and seamy side of contemporary society. Towards the end of the Tang Dynasty famous poets, like Du Mu (803-853) and Li Shangyin (813-858), each with his distinctive style, reflected the sufferings of the people in their writings.

The great thinker and writer Han Yu (768-824) advocated plain literary composition instead of the *pian* style of writing — a style in which all sentences run strictly in pairs. He propagated Confucianism in opposition to Buddhism and Taoism — the latter two, like the *pian* style of writing, had been in vogue since the time of the Southern and Northern dynasties. A revolutionary in the literature and thought of the time, Han Yu was a pioneer of the free style of prose composition which was widely adopted under Northern Song. He was also one of the forerunners of rational philosophy or neo-Confucianism, which flourished in the Northern Song period and afterwards.

During the Tang Dynasty art reached a very high level, and there was a galaxy of great painters and sculptors. The figure paintings of Wu Daozi, the landscapes of Wang Wei (699-759), and the multitude of mural paintings preserved in the grottoes of Dunhuang, all produced during the Tang Dynasty, will remain landmarks in the history of Chinese art. The sculpture of Yang Huizhi is renowned for its tremendous fidelity to life both in form and expression. Magnificent specimens of Tang sculpture are still preserved intact at Dunhuang. Music and dancing also flourished.

There were many and varied forms of religious beliefs during this period. Zoroastrianism was introduced into China during the Northern Dynasties. Nestorianism,

Islamism and Manichaeanism were introduced successively during the Tang Dynasty, but the most widely-held faiths were Taoism and Buddhism, especially the latter. Buddhism spread far and wide during Tang and several sects arose, the most flourishing being the Dhyana sect. Devout and learned monks travelled to distant India to study Buddhist sutras. Hsuan Tsang (596-664) and Yi Ching (635-713) were the most famous of these monks. They translated many of the Buddhist sutras brought back from India.

Buddhism in the Tang Dynasty had its material as well as its spiritual influence on the lives of the people. The Buddhist monasteries received donations of land and orchards and, by seizure or other means of appropriation, acquired large estates, farms and water mills. They also carried out a system of usury among the peasants. The exemption of the monasteries from taxes affected the revenue of the state so seriously during the reign of Emperor Wu Zong (841-846) that a decree was issued ordering the monks to return to secular life. But when Xuan Zong (reigned 847-859) ascended the throne, they were allowed to return to the temples, and Buddhism recovered its original privileged position.

The Unification of China Under the Song Dynasty (960-1126) In 960 Zhao Kuangyin (927-976), a military officer of the Later Zhou Dynasty, organized a mutiny, captured political power from the ruling house and founded the Song Dynasty with its capital at Kaifeng (in Henan). This is known in history as the Northern Song Dynasty.

The states of Jingnan, Shu, Southern Han, Southern Tang and Wuyue (of the Ten States) were subjugated in the early years of this dynasty. The state which held out the longest was Northern Han in northern Shanxi.

The elimination of all these states ended the division that had existed under the Five Dynasties and Ten States.

Zhao Kuangyin, later known as Emperor Tai Zu of Song, saw political unification as the most pressing need of the country and laid down a policy to prevent internal dissension among the members of the ruling class so that he might be free to suppress any resistance on the part of the people. The new dynasty's policy on external affairs was entirely defensive.

Although not a powerful dynasty, the Song government was more centralized than Tang. The administration of the latter retained the marks of an aristocracy, while the Song government was organized on strictly bureaucratic lines, both in military and financial affairs. Supreme control over army affairs was vested in the central Privy Council. Local finances were entrusted to commissioners appointed by the central government.

The Song rulers adopted measures to facilitate the recovery of the rural economy, such as improvement of irrigation and the encouragement of land reclamation. Nevertheless, the countryside was in a state of prostration, mainly because, in consequence of the defeat of the peasant wars, there had been no change in the tremendous concentration of land which had prevailed since Tang and the Five Dynasties. The greater part of the arable land of the country was still held by the nobles, officials, landlords and merchants who neither paid taxes nor contributed any kind of labour service. These big landlords were called "official households" or "influential households". Buddhist monks and nuns and Taoist priests were also exempted from taxation and labour service. They were designated respectively as Buddhist followers' households and Taoist followers' households. The peasants holding small plots of land, craftsmen, and the middle and petty traders bore the brunt of taxation.

The Development of Industry and Trade Gold, silver, copper, iron ore, tin and lead were mined on a large scale during the Song Dynasty. Coal was widely used as fuel and also for the smelting of iron, and more than two hundred enterprises were concerned with mining and metallurgy. The technique of shipbuilding made great progress and ships with paddle-wheels propelled by manpower were used for military purposes. The compass was already used by navigators and gunpowder was used in warfare. The technique of spinning and weaving, the manufacture of paper and lacquer-ware, the art of printing which had been invented during the Sui and Tang dynasties, and the manufacture of porcelain which had been improved in the Jin period, were all further developed.

Thousands of workers were employed in the government-operated smelting works, cotton mills and armouries, the majority of the workers being wage-labourers.

The cities and towns which had begun to flourish during the Five Dynasties and Ten States became more prosperous. Some city dealers in tea, salt and rice boasted fortunes of one hundred thousand or several million "strings of cash".

During the reign of Zhen Zong (reigned 998-1022) paper money was issued in various forms. Promise-to-pay notes came into use and circulated as paper money.

The Reforms Introduced by Wang Anshi and His Failure The appropriation of land by the bits landholders, taxation, usury and labour service undermined the rural economy. The enormous tribute which the Song paid to Khitan and Western Xia from the beginning of the reign of Zhen Zong was a particularly heavy burden which the peasantry were forced to shoulder. There were widespread peasant hunger riots during Ren Zong's reign (1023-63) following a great famine in Hebei and Shandong. At the same time the menace from Khitan grew, and by the time Shen Zong (reigned 1066-85) ascended the throne, the Song Dynasty was facing both an internal and an external crisis. Reforms introduced by Wang Anshi (1019-86) were the logical sequence to this situation.

This outstanding Chinese statesman recognized the root cause of the trouble, and set about the introduction of reforms, which he proceeded to resolutely enforce. The reforms, a reflection of the political demands of the peasants, handicraftsmen, petty traders and small landlords, were directed against the big landlords and big merchants. For example, his Law of Land Measurement and Equitable Taxation was designed to compel tax-evading landlords to pay in accordance with the size of their holdings. His Equitable Distribution Law was designed to prevent wealthy merchants and big traders from taking advantage of the crisis of the state and the common people's distress. His Young Crops Law, which provided for low-interest loans from the government to the peasants, was calculated to restrain the landlords and wealthy merchants from taking advantage of the difficulties of the peasants during the lean period before harvest and demanding exorbitant rates of interest on borrowed money. His Service-Exemption Law compelled big landlords, who performed no labour service for the government before, to contribute money instead. His

Trade Law was intended to restrain unscrupulous merchants from manipulating commodity prices.

Wang Anshi also introduced laws dealing with the organization of the militia and for the breeding of horses for military use. He reorganized the army, equipped it with new weapons, and established thirty-six garrison posts north of the Huanghe River to strengthen national defence. His purpose was to place some check on the big landlords and merchants, stave off the impending open class conflict, and to concentrate on the building up of defensive measures against Khitan and Western Xia.

The big landlords and merchants, including typical representatives of the landowning class like Sima Guang (1019-86), violently opposed the reforms. Emperor Shen Zong had not been dead very long when the reform laws were repealed. Later the ministers under Hui Zong (reigned 1101-25) also advocated reforms and "new laws" were introduced which cloaked the intensified exploitation of the peasantry and served rather than curtailed the interests of the big landlords. As a result, there was another series of peasant uprisings, under the leadership of Song Jiang and Fang La (?-1121).

The Fall of Northern Song Throughout the 320 years of the rule of the Song some border tribes in the north rose and grew strong. The Khitan were the first, and they were followed by the Nüzhen, and later the Mongols.

The founder of the Song Dynasty and his successors adhered to a policy of external appeasement and internal repression, dissipating national resources on the suppression of their own people. They continually ceded territory, paid tribute to the border tribes and sued for peace on the most humiliating terms.

The peace signed by Song with the Liao (Khitan) in 1004 was the first in a series of acts of national disgrace. Thenceforth the Song rulers bought temporary peace by handing over an annual tribute of 100,000 ounces of silver and 200,000 rolls of silk to the Khitan.

Simultaneously with the invasion of the Khitan, a branch of the Qiang people occupied the regions embracing modern Ningxia, Gansu and northern Shaanxi and established the Kingdom of Western Xia (1038-1227). They made frequent incursions into the northwestern regions. The Song government also tried to conciliate them with gifts of silver and silk.

In 1115 the Nüzhen rose in the Heilongjiang River valley in the northeast and founded the Kingdom of Jin (1115-1234). The Song rulers co-operated with them in attacking Khitan, hoping to take back Yanjing with their assistance. The Nüzhen conquered the Khitan but, instead of restoring Yanjing to Song, they occupied the city.

The Nüzhen then swept southward to overthrow Song. The Song Emperor Hui Zong and his ruling clique had degenerated through luxurious living. To them, the planting of rare flowers and the decoration of their palaces and gardens were more important than preparations against invasion. In 1126 when the Nüzhen seized the Song capital, Kaifeng, they captured two Song emperors — Hui Zong, who had then abdicated, and his successor, his son Qin Zong. The Northern Song Dynasty came to an end.

The Establishment of the Southern Song Dynasty (1127-1279) In 1127 a group of civil and military officials led by Emperor Gao Zong (reigned 1127-62), another son of Hui Zong, crossed the Changjiang River and established a new government at Linan (Hangzhou), which is historically known as the Southern Song Dynasty.

The Huanghe River basin was then continually being invaded by the Nüzhen, and the peasants were often in armed conflict with them. One of the Song commanders, the national hero Yue Fei (1103-41), led an army which dealt a head-on blow against the Nüzhen. The Southern Song government, dominated by a group of capitulationists headed by Qin Hui, had already presented Nüzhen with a stretch of territory lying north of the Huai River and extending westward to the Dasanguan Pass, hoping thereby to obtain a temporary peace south of Changjiang. These defeatists now sought to appease the enemy by refusing to support the armed forces of the peasants behind the enemy lines, killed Yue Fei and then withdrew the Song troops from the front.

The Nüzhen, however, did not abandon their attack and in 1161 they carried the war right up to the banks of the Changjiang River. It was only after persistent resistance by the people and by the armed forces of the south that Southern Song eventually succeeded in stabilizing its rule in the Changjiang basin. The officials, landlords and merchants had meanwhile fled in large numbers to the south, taking with them their degenerate practices and imposing heavy labour service and taxation on the people there.

After the removal of the political centre to the south, Linan, the capital of Southern Song, rapidly developed into a populous metropolitan city. Many other big cities and towns also rose. For example, in the prefecture of Jiankang (modern Nanjing), there were fourteen towns and more than twenty markets during Northern Song. They now became even more prosperous. Guangzhou,

Mingzhou (Ningbo, Zhejiang) and Quanzhou (Jinjiang, Fujian) developed as ports for overseas trade, where commissioners were stationed in charge of commercial affairs and for the collection of revenue. Many foreign merchants came to trade, and in Guangzhou a foreign quarter was established as an exclusive residential district for them. Chengdu, Jiangling and Suzhou were prosperous inland commercial cities, where handicraft workshops flourished. Marked technical progress was made by government and private handicrafts in the manufacture of gunpowder, arms, and the building of ocean-going ships as well as in the making of cloth. Kapok was grown in Fujian, Guangdong and Guangxi and its cultivation was extended to the middle and lower reaches of Changjiang, and so another fabric was added to the existing list of textiles.

The Fall of Southern Song The Mongols, a nomadic people living in the Onon valley in northeastern Mongolia, rose in 1206 under their leader, Genghis Khan (1155-1227), and became a world-shaking power. In the three decades from 1218 to 1253, they swept across the world like a tornado. They conquered the various states of the Western Regions as well as Western Xia, and then advanced further into the west, annexing the whole of Central Asia, Russia and many Eastern European countries. In 1234 they destroyed the Nüzhen's rule in China.

For the next forty-six years Southern Song was under constant threat of conquest by the Mongols. The Mongols resorted to a circuitous strategy, and before making a frontal attack their troops penetrated through the occupied Qinghai grasslands, Yunnan and Tibet. Then they advanced into Sichuan. In 1276, under the command of Kublai Khan (reigned 1260-94), later known as Emperor Shi Zu of the Yuan Dynasty, the Mongols conquered the capital of Southern Song, Linan. The people and armies of Southern Song, led by three national heroes, Wen Tianxiang (1236-82), Zhang Shijie (?-1279) and Lu Xiufu (1238-79), resisted bitterly but were eventually defeated by the overwhelming forces of the enemy. In 1279 the Mongols occupied Guangdong and destroyed the last contingent of the Southern Song army, bringing the whole of China under their control.

Printing and the Advance of Culture The invention of printing was one of the most important events which took place in the Sui and Tang dynasties with worldwide repercussions. It greatly facilitated the spread and development of culture everywhere.

Previously, all Chinese books had been copied by hand. By the end of the sixth century printed matter was being produced from engraved wooden blocks. During the years 860-873 (in the Tang Dynasty), beautiful woodblock printings of dictionaries and almanacs and Buddhist scriptures were in circulation. The technique of engraving made further progress and more engraved wooden blocks were being used by the time of the Five Dynasties, and in 932 the government of Later Tang printed the Nine Classics of the Confucian school. In the areas south of Changjiang, and especially in Sichuan, numerous books were printed from wood blocks. In 981 the Buddhist *Tripitaka*, comprising 5,048 volumes, was available in a printed edition.

The technique of printing reached a high degree of perfection during the reign of Ren Zong (1023-63) of the Song Dynasty. Bi Sheng invented a movable type made of clay, and after that many voluminous works such as the *Tai Ping Reign-Period Imperial Encyclopaedia*, *Anthology from the End of the Liang Dynasty*, and *Col-*

lection of Material on the Lives of Emperors and Ministers, each consisting of 1,000 volumes, were printed. With the introduction of printed books, rectangular thread-sewn volumes took the place of the former manuscript rolls, and there was a great increase in the publication of books. The Northern Song government had a library of over 70,000 volumes. Some private collections in the early years of Southern Song contained more than 100,000 volumes.

This increase in the number of books naturally led to the general spread of knowledge and to progress in various special branches of learning. The *Pharmacopoeia,* compiled during the reign of Hui Zong of Song, lists 893 medicinal herbs and describes their properties. The *Treatise on Architectural Methods,* compiled by Li Jie about the same time, gives a detailed account of Chinese buildings, complete with diagrams and descriptions of building materials and colours. This book is a comprehensive description of Chinese architecture from the Tang Dynasty to the period of Northern Song. *A Collection of the Most Important Military Techniques,* compiled during the reign of Ren Zong of Song, contains a section which details the making of gunpowder.

The birth of a new school of Confucian philosophy, known as rational philosophy or neo-Confucianism, was a noteworthy development in the field of social science. It reflected the influence of Buddhist philosophy, particularly that of the Dhyana sect of Buddhism. In other words, Confucianism had become more metaphysical. Cheng Yi (1033-1107) and Zhu Xi (1130-1200) were great neo-Confucianists. There were also notable advances in the art of recording historical events. The *New History of the Five Dynasties* by Ouyang Xiu (1007-72),

Mirror of History by Sima Guang (1019-86), *Historical Collections* by Zheng Qiao (1104-62) and *Record of Events of the Mirror of History* by Yuan Shu (1131-1205) are all acknowledged authoritative historical works.

The main contribution of Song literature was *ci*, a new form of poetic composition. Although subject to limitations of tone and rhyme, the lines vary in length and are therefore more adapted to the expression of emotions than the previous style of verse-writing. The two Song dynasties produced many notable *ci* poets, among the best known being Xin Qiji (1139-1207) and the poetess Li Qingzhao (1081-?).

The Establishment of the Yuan Dynasty (1271-1368)

Kublai Khan founded the Yuan Dynasty in 1271 and conquered Southern Song in 1279. Throughout the eighty-nine years of Mongol rule the people of Han and other nationalities suffered both national and class oppression.

The Yuan Dynasty divided people into four classes. The Mongols comprised the first class and were treated as privileged persons. Next on the social scale came the Semu people (from the Western Regions), who were followed by the Han people, the southern Han being regarded as the lowest class.

The Han, including the southerners, were excluded from positions of command in the national armed forces and also from most of the high administrative posts. They could become local officials, but must be under the supervision of a Mongol or a Semu overseer. They were forbidden to keep weapons without first obtaining permission.

During the period when China was under the unified rule of Kublai Khan, agricultural production was restored and even developed to some extent in the north. But on the whole the rule of the Mongol aristocrats hindered the growth of China's social economy.

The Mongols seized land in a more ruthless way than ever before witnessed in Chinese history. Huge tracts of public land north of Huanghe were converted into pastures. Land was also seized south of Huanghe but the treatment was not so drastic as on the other side of the river. The situation south of Changjiang remained as it had been under Southern Song.

The government and public land confiscated from the Khitan and Southern Song was distributed among the Mongol nobles. The grants ranged from 20 *qing*[1] up to 5,000 *qing*. The arable land of the peasants was also seized in various districts and allotted to Mongol garrisons for cultivation or bestowed on monasteries. During the reign of the Yuan Emperor Wu Zong (1308-11) there were two hundred "garrison fields" covering a total of 172,000 *qing* of land. The amount of land granted to monasteries was fabulous, as can be seen from the gift of 162,000 *qing* to the Husheng Monastery by Emperor Shun Di (1333-68). Princes, officials and priests unrestrainedly seized land belonging to the common people and converted it into pastures or rented it out for cultivation. Han landowners in the middle and lower Changjiang regions also appropriated land without hindrance. In some districts five-sixths of all the arable land was owned by landlords, the largest of whom collected an annual rent of 200,000 or 300,000 *shi*[2] and commanded the labour of as many as ten thousand peasant families.

---

[1] A *qing* = 100 mu, or 6.66 hectares or 16.47 acres.

[2] A *shi* is about a picul of grain.

The Yuan rulers robbed the peasants of their horses for military purposes in addition to seizing their land, and it is estimated that 700,000 horses were taken away from the peasants during this shortlived dynasty. These animals had been used by northern peasants for drawing carts and ploughs, and agricultural production suffered seriously as a result. Large numbers of carts and boats were also commandeered, and these two factors created considerable transport difficulties in the countryside.

The peasants' loss of land, horses, carts and boats was accompanied by loss of personal freedom, and the majority of those living in the north were enslaved by the Mongol nobles and forced to till land or tend cattle and sheep without remuneration. In the south most of the peasants became the tenants of big landlords and were compelled to pay a rent far heavier than the land tax. They were also obliged to perform different kinds of labour service. In some districts the landlords were empowered to sell their tenants like slaves or rent them out to other landlords.

Peasants who managed to retain their own land had to pay land and poll taxes. The land tax was three *sheng* of grain per mu and the poll tax was three *shi* of grain per person. South of Changjiang this payment could be made by a combination of rice and cash — one-third in rice and the balance in cash. Labour service could also be commuted into payment in silk and silver. This heavy taxation and forced labour service made many landed peasants surrender their land to Mongol nobles and become their tenants.

Industry and Trade in the Yuan Dynasty While agriculture declined, handicraft industries providing consumer goods for the aristocracy developed considerably. This was especially true of handicrafts under state management which had attained a high degree of specialization. There were workshops for the making of articles of gold, silver, brass, iron, bamboo, wood, jade, stone and glazed porcelain. There were also brick kilns, tanneries and armouries. Iron-smelting was divided into two branches, one for iron smelting and the other for steel making. The tanning industry was subdivided into three parts for tanning, bating and shaving. The arms industry had separate sections for the manufacture of bows, bow strings, arrows, armour and saddles.

Privately-owned handicraft enterprises in the cities were equally well developed. According to the *Travels* of Marco Polo, there were many fairly large private workshops in the city of Hangzhou. Thousands of workers employed in government handicraft workshops and armouries sank to the status of slave-labour, payment being barely enough to keep body and soul together. They were called government or military artisans. Hired hands, known as civilian artisans, also existed.

During the reign of Kublai Khan, the Huitong Canal was dug in what is now Shandong Province. Guo Shoujing (1231-1316), the outstanding scientist of the Yuan Dynasty, was responsible for the project of the Tonghui Canal (from Tongzhou to Beijing) which completed the Grand Canal, linking Beijing with the most prosperous southern city of Hangzhou. This Grand Canal greatly facilitated communication between the north and the south. A water route from Changjiang to the mouth of Baihe, round the Shandong Peninsula, was also opened to shipping. Paper money was issued on a colossal scale. Guangzhou, Quanzhou, Qingyuan (Ningbo), Shanghai, Ganpu, Wenzhou and Hangzhou developed as centres of maritime trade. Inland communication was facilitated by courier stations and stagecoaches. Many Westerners came to China, bringing with them Western merchandise and Western culture. These foreigners also carried Chinese culture to the West. Marco Polo, a Venetian who spent fifteen years in the service of the Grand Khan, lauded and publicized the wealth and splendours of China when he returned to Europe. Westerners became envious and sought to acquire Chinese culture and civilization.

Literature and Religion in the Yuan Dynasty The drama, known as *za ju,* reached a very high level of development during the Yuan Dynasty. According to historical records of Yuan, there were more than a hundred playwrights, including Guan Hanqing, Wang Shifu and Ma Zhiyuan, and a number of Mongols. The writing of novels flourished, the best-known novel of that period being *Outlaws of the Marsh* by Shi Naian.

Influenced by Han culture, the Mongols and Semu people did well in literature. The Mongols adopted a liberal attitude towards religion. They were devout Buddhists and held the lamas in great reverence, but tolerated the spread and propagation of Islam and Nestorian Christianity. But occasionally they assumed a hostile attitude towards Taoism.

The Great Peasant Uprisings Against the Rule of the Mongol Nobles in China The Yuan Dynasty reached the apex of its power during the reign of Kublai Khan. After his death it began to decline. Violent quarrels about succession arose among the imperial princes and coups d'état frequently occurred. The internal conflicts of the ruling class reached a critical stage and, in the period between 1307 and 1333, a succession of eight emperors occupied the throne. The tyranny and exactions of the nobles, the officials and the powerful landlords were coupled with flood and drought and famine. Life became unbearable for the Han people. A great uprising of peasants took place during the reign of the last Yuan emperor, Shun Di.

The armed struggles of the Han peasants against Yuan rule had been in progress from the time of the fall of Southern Song. In the north, the peasants banded together and, under the name of the White Lotus Sect, took part in many uprisings. In the south the number of peasant rebellions was even greater. *The History of the Yuan Dynasty* states: "During the ten years after the submission of the regions south of Changjiang there were two hundred localities where brigands and robbers rose up in arms." This book also records: "Over four hundred places south of Changjiang were infested with brigands and robbers." These uprisings were crushed, but there was another upsurge in the peasant movement in 1351, when Liu Futong (?-1363), Xu Shouhui (?-1360), and Guo Zixing (?-1355) raised the standard of rebellion. This was followed by those led by Chen Youliang (1320-63), Zhang Shicheng (1321-67) and others. The whole of Huanghe, Huaihe, and Changjiang valleys became involved in peasant wars against the Yuan rulers and their accomplices, the feudal landlords of the Han nationality. These wars lasted nearly twenty years, during which rival leaders split up the country into many sections, each trying to maintain his own independent regime. Finally Zhu Yuanzhang (1328-98), a commander under Guo Zixing, succeeded in overthrowing Yuan rule, vanquished all his rivals, and established the Ming Dynasty.

IV. THE MING AND QING DYNASTIES (14th to 19th Century)

The Ming Dynasty (1368-1644) The Ming Dynasty, with Nanjing as its capital, was founded in 1368. As Emperor Tai Zu of Ming, Zhu Yuanzhang sent his troops to drive the Yuan Emperor Shun Di and the Mongol nobles out of Beijing and thus ended the cruel rule of the Yuan Dynasty. A powerful and prosperous dynasty had come into being.

After driving out the Mongol nobles, Zhu Yuanzhang eliminated rival rebel leaders and killed many of his own generals whom he suspected of plotting against him. He concentrated all power in his own hands and exercised an extremely despotic and centralized rule. He separated military and political affairs, and vested administration in the hands of the ministers of six boards who were directly responsible to him.

After the death of Zhu Yuanzhang, his fourth son, later known as Emperor Cheng Zu (1360-1424), seized the throne from his nephew, Jian Wen Di, and moved the capital to Beijing. During the reign of Cheng Zu and Xuan Zong the dynasty reached the zenith of its power. An armed fleet under the command of Zheng He (1371-1435), a court eunuch, made seven voyages of exploration to the South Sea Islands and the Indian Ocean, succeeded in establishing good trading and cultural relations with the inhabitants and laid the foundations for Chinese settlers who subsequently helped local inhabitants in their economic development. Zheng He also sailed as far as the eastern shores of Africa.

During the first fifty years of the Ming Dynasty armies were sent several times to attack Mongolia in order to prevent the Mongol nobles from essaying a return. None of these expeditions gained decisive victories. In 1449 Emperor Ying Zong went to the frontier and personally directed a resistance against the Mongols. The Mongol armies defeated the Ming troops and captured the emperor. The Ming Dynasty held the Mongols in hostility for a long time. To maintain direct control over the border tribes in northeast China, the early Ming rulers established military districts and garrisons and other administrative setups there. For instance, there was once a military district in today's Koumiaojie area in Heilongjiang Province, and a garrison in Jianzhou in modern Jilin Province.

Concentration of Land and the Beginning of Money Rent

When Zhu Yuanzhang drove out the Mongols he instituted various measures favourable to the restoration and development of the social economy. Land reclamation was encouraged, irrigation was improved, and the cotton-growing areas were extended. There was a reduction in taxes, some exemption of land rent, and a free distribution of seeds. As a result land, which had been laid waste by the wars in the provinces of Shandong, Hebei, Henan and in the Huaihe River valley, was again planted with cereals and other crops.

During the Ming Dynasty, the emperors, nobles and officials all tried to seize land and create large estates, and at one time the imperial house owned 37,000 *qing* of farm land. Some favoured relatives of the emperor and court eunuchs owned between them 332 farms, a total of 33,000 *qing* of land. Two princes, Lu and Fu, owned 40,000 *qing* and 20,000 *qing* of land respectively. The farms of dukes, marquises and ministers usually consisted of about 100 *qing* of land each, plus frequent enlargements by purchase, through imperial grants, or by forcible seizure. Most of the landlords engaged in the appropriation of land. To quote Gu Yanwu (1613-82), a patriotic scholar who lived during the closing years of the Ming Dynasty: "One-tenth of the people of Wu (Suzhou) owned land and the rest were landless." This shows how land was concentrated in the hands of a few people towards the end of the Ming Dynasty.

At this period land was mainly divided into two categories: government land and people's land. The former constituted one-seventh of the total arable land of the country. In Suzhou and Songjiang, the government held fifteen plots of land to every one held by the people. Land tax on government land was 5.3 *sheng* per mu and on the people's land it was 3.3 *sheng* per mu. There were other categories of land called "heavy-rent-land" and confiscated land, the tax on these being much heavier. In certain districts it was four *dou*[1] or as high as one *shi* per mu.

Land tax, collected twice a year, in summer and autumn, might be paid in kind or in silver or paper money. During the reign of Emperor Shen Zong taxes, labour service and other levies were combined into a single tax, payable in silver, the actual amount depending on the size of the land holdings. This was done under what came to be known as the All-in-One Law, which introduced money rent into China.

Growth of Handicraft Workshops, Prosperity of Urban Economy and Arrival of Europeans The Ming Dynasty surpassed all previous dynasties in the development of handicrafts, principally because of the emancipation of

[1] A *dou* is one-tenth of a *shi*, or a picul.

the artisans from a position of quasi-slavery. A secondary reason was the transmission of many handicraft techniques from the Western Regions during the Yuan Dynasty.

Iron-smelting, shipbuilding, spinning and weaving, printing, and the production of lacquer-ware and porcelain all made marked technical advances.

A considerable amount of technical skill and equipment was required for the operation of enterprises such as the iron works at Zunhua in Hebei Province, the printing shops at Bilin (Wujin, Jiangsu) and Suzhou which used movable lead or wooden type, the textile mills of Suzhou and Hangzhou, the glass-making workshops of Yidu in Shandong, the shipyards of Guangdong and Fujian, and particularly the porcelain potteries of Jingdezhen in Jiangxi, where tens of thousands of pieces were turned out every year, and a record of 159,000 pieces was achieved in 1591. These handicrafts could no longer be carried on by individuals or in individual households, and generally took the form of workshop production. Their mode of production contained the germs of capitalism. Just as it can be said that Western Zhou marked the beginning of feudalism, China can be described as having entered the last phase of feudalism by the middle of the Ming Dynasty.

As a result of Zhu Yuanzhang's order to the farmers that they must grow cotton, spinning and weaving of cotton became the most important subsidiary occupation of the peasants. And from the beginning of the sixteenth century, traders established direct connections with rural spinners and weavers, placing orders with them. By the beginning of the next century peasant spinners and weavers in certain districts were able to obtain equipment and raw materials from the traders, and thus became wage-earners.

The craftsmen began to form guilds for the protection of their common interests but mainly for the protection of the special rights of the guild masters. The guilds also served the government in such matters as the enrolling of workers and the collection of tributes.

During the Ming Dynasty thirty-three great commercial cities sprang up, including Beijing and Nanjing. Eight of them were located in the north, and eleven in the provinces of Zhejiang and Jiangsu.

Merchants had also their own organizations. Some were guilds, open to those engaged in the same trade; others were hostels which received people hailing from the same province or city. Both were developed from the guilds of the Tang and Song dynasties.

Overseas trade reached a new high level in the early years of Ming. Portuguese trading ships arrived in Guangdong in 1516 and inaugurated a sea route between China and Europe. Spanish traders, who came in 1557, were followed by the Dutch in 1606 and the English in 1637.

Catholic missionaries came in the wake of the traders. In 1581 an Italian Jesuit missionary, Matteo Ricci (1552-1610), arrived in Guangdong to propagate his faith. He arrived in Beijing in 1610, and was soon followed by many more Catholic missionaries.

Peasant Wars and the Fall of the Ming Dynasty The full flowering period of Ming rule lasted about sixty years. The century following the reign of Shi Zong, from 1521 to 1627, witnessed its rapid decline. The Tartars invaded the country from the northwest, and Japanese pirates harassed the southeast. After 1616, when the Manchus established their kingdom, the threat from the northeast became serious.

The court in Beijing was dominated by eunuchs. They excluded all political opponents from office and were in turn opposed by a group of literati known as the Dong Lin party. The internal strife in the ranks of the ruling class spread rapidly and the political situation worsened. The civil administration became riddled with corruption, and forced levies and imposts made the people desperate. Under the pretext of strengthening the defences of Liaodong against the Manchus, the government imposed a new tax, placing yet another heavy burden on the people, and peasant revolts broke out in 1628.

The first of these uprisings was in northern Shaanxi, where a severe famine was raging. The peasants, the soldiers of the frontier defence army, and the unemployed couriers were reduced to hunger and desperation. The troops garrisoned at Yanan and Suide mutinied and later joined hands with the peasants in raising the flag of rebellion. Li Zicheng (1606-45) of Mizhi and Zhang Xianzhong (1606-46) of Yanan were the foremost leaders of this hunger revolt of the peasants. In 1635 the leaders held a great rebel conclave at Yingyang in Henan; members of thirteen clans and seventy-two military units attended.

Zhang Xianzhong led his troops from Henan, Anhui, Hubei and Hunan into Sichuan. The peasant army of Li Zicheng crossed the Huanghe River into Shaanxi in 1644, and moved northward. After passing through Taiyuan, Datong and the Juyongguan Pass, it entered Beijing. The last emperor of the Ming Dynasty, Chong Zhen (1628-44), who was unable to get out of the city, hanged himself at Jingshan (Coal Hill) behind the imperial palace. The Ming Dynasty ended with his death.

The New Spirit in Ming Culture By the middle of the Ming period the neo-Confucianism of the school of Cheng Yi and Zhu Xi, which had been officially supported and blessed by the rulers of the three dynasties of Song, Yuan and Ming, had become decadent, and had fallen into disrepute among a section of the literati. A new school was founded by Wang Shouren (1472-1528), advocating "the unity of knowledge with practice" as a protest against the hypocrisy and pedantry of the Cheng-Zhu school. Wang Shouren was the most important neo-Confucianist of the Ming era. His subjective idealism dominated the teaching of the period from the middle of the Ming Dynasty to the early years of the Qing Dynasty. Two other schools of thought also opposed the emptiness and fatuity of the Cheng-Zhu school. The first, known as the school of universal learning, was in favour of the widest possible reading of books. The other school stressed the necessity for the study of history and the classics, with a view to their practical application to political and social problems. The most advanced branch of the latter school was also interested in the study of natural science. In this connection Song Yingxing's *Nature Develops Resources* and Li Shizhen's (1518-93) *Compendium of Materia Medica* deserve special mention. The first named work explains the processes of industrial manufacture in great detail, while the second, dealing with zoology, botany and mineralogy, shows some systematization in classifying plants.

Western learning in such sciences as mathematics, astronomy, calendar-making, water conservancy, mechanics, geography and physiology was introduced to China during the Ming period, and Chinese scholars like Xu Guangqi (1562-1633) and Li Zhizao (?-1630) had begun their studies along Western scientific lines. Sprouts of capitalism appeared during the Ming Dynasty, and the new culture was a result of the new economic elements in society.

New achievements were added to the credit of literature. The more accomplished *nan qu*, southern drama, replaced the *za ju* (the northern), as the main current in play-writing. Characteristic of this period were novels written in vernacular, such as the *Romance of the Three Kingdoms, Journey to the West, Canonization of the Gods* and *The Golden Lotus.*

The Entry of the Manchus Through the Shanhaiguan Pass and the Han People's Struggle Against the Manchus

The Manchus, a branch of the Nüzhen, originally dwelt at the confluence of the Mudan and Sungari rivers, where their main occupations were agriculture and livestock-breeding. They were culturally backward.

In the 1580s the Manchus, under their chief Nurhachi, annexed several other tribes and became powerful. Nurhachi had set up the state of Jin in 1616; its name was later changed to Qing. This state gradually extended from the Suzi River valley to that of the Dalin River.

In 1621 Nurhachi, later known as Emperor Tai Zu of Qing, seized the Ming city of Liaoyang and made it his capital. Later he moved the capital to Shenyang. He died in 1626 and was succeeded by his son, Emperor Tai Zong. The new ruler conquered Mongolia and by continuous warfare seized many cities and rural areas in the northeast. When the peasant leader Li Zicheng entered Beijing the vanguard of Tai Zong's troops was rapidly approaching the Shanhaiguan Pass, where the

Great Wall meets the sea. Wu Sangui, the Ming garrison commander of the pass, betrayed his people and led the Manchu troops through the Great Wall. The Manchu Emperor Tai Zong had died and had been succeeded by his son Fu Lin. The Manchus, with the traitor Wu Sangui and his troops as guides, defeated Li Zicheng's peasant army and occupied Beijing. Fu Lin proclaimed himself emperor of China and became known as Emperor Shi Zu of Qing (reigned 1644-61).

Large numbers of the civil and military officials of the Ming court went over to the side of the Qing rulers and made frantic efforts to serve their new masters by helping to suppress the resistance of their Han compatriots. Some of the Ming nobles and officials, however, fought against the Manchus with the support of the people. In these wars of resistance renowned national heroes like Shi Kefa (?-1645) and Zheng Chenggong, known abroad as Koxinga (1624-62), Li Zicheng's officers Li Jin (?-1649) and Li Laiheng (?-1664), and Zhang Xianzhong's officer Li Dingguo (?-1662) played their part. Li Dingguo held the southwest against the Manchus for thirteen years, carrying on a war of resistance until the last inch of territory was lost. Zheng Chenggong continued the war against the Manchus on Taiwan, and it was not until 1683, twenty years after his death, that the Manchu forces eventually occupied that island.

Prosperity of the Qing Dynasty and Its Decline (1636-1912) The Qing Dynasty reached the zenith of its power during the first one and half centuries of its existence. Ruling China with a small number of Manchu nobles, but fearful of the Han people's resistance, it dared not pursue an extreme policy of exploitation. The productive forces of society continued to develop, the rural economy prospered and more land was brought under cultivation. The population grew to 400 million, and state revenue increased. During the reigns of Emperor Kang Xi (1662-1722) and Emperor Qian Long (1736-95) the unity of China was further strengthened.

At the end of the 17th century the Qing government had launched three expeditions against the Dzungars and suppressed their rebellions. It sent its troops to escort the Sixth Dalai Lama back to Lhasa, the sacred city of Lamaism. The Qing government, defining the functions and organization of the local government of Tibet, decreed in 1726 that high commissioners should be stationed in Tibet as the highest administrative officials. The central government thus exercised full authority over Tibet.

The reign of Emperor Qian Long marked the heyday of the Qing Dynasty. After 1756 Qing troops subdued the Dzungars and the Uygurs (Uighurs) in Xinjiang. Meanwhile, the Qing government reinforced its troops in Tibet and strengthened the power of its commissioners there. As a result, it consolidated its rule over Tibet and Xinjiang.

The last years of the reign of Qian Long were marked by misrule and corruption, and when his successor Jia Qing (reigned 1796-1820) ascended the throne, the various oppressed peoples, mainly the Han, were in revolt, and the dynasty was on the road to decline.

In 1774 Wang Lun, a peasant leader in Shandong, unfurled the banner of rebellion against the Manchus. This was quickly followed by uprisings of the Hui people in Gansu and of the Miao people in Hunan and Guizhou provinces. During the reign of Jia Qing, two secret societies, the White Lotus Sect and the Heavenly Reason

Sect, led peasant revolts. The White Lotus Sect rebellion lasted nine years and spread through Hebei, Sichuan and Shaanxi. It greatly weakened the rule of the Qing Dynasty. In the south, the Heaven and Earth Society and the Society of Elder Brothers staged uprisings in numerous places. These local uprisings continued and spread and, towards the end of the reign of Dao Guang (1821-50), the great peasant revolution of the Taiping Heavenly Kingdom broke out.

The Qing Institutions The political organization of the Qing Dynasty was largely modelled upon the Ming system but was more highly centralized. Its central administration was led by a Grand Council, which transacted the military and political affairs and worked under the direct supervision of the emperor. The job of the ministers of state was to carry out the orders of this Grand Council.

An extremely repressive policy was carried out against the conquered Han people. Garrisons of the Eight Banners (Manchu troops) and Green Battalions (of Han origin) were stationed at all strategic points and military control was established throughout the country. The Qing government tried to suppress anti-Manchu ideas by persecuting many Han writers on the pretext that they used improper language against the Manchus. The men of Han were allowed to hold posts as central or district government officials, but certain positions were barred to them. Although national discrimination against the Han was not so open as under the Mongols, the measures adopted against them were far more stringent and extensive.

The Qing rulers, like the Yuan rulers, seized land without restraint, and all the farm land belonging to the Ming imperial house and nobles was confiscated.

Part was taken over by the Manchu imperial family and the rest given to Manchu princes and the soldiers of the Eight Banners. According to the *Statutes of the Qing Dynasty* and *A Digest of Documents and Records of the Qing Dynasty,* the imperial house owned 868 farms and the imperial clansmen of the Eight Banners owned 1,407 large farms, 259 small farms, 375 large orchards and 102 small orchards. The garrisons of the Eight Banners occupied more than three million mu of land for stabling and other military purposes.

At the beginning of their rule, the Manchus followed the All-in-One Law taxation system introduced by Ming. In 1725 they combined the poll tax and other miscellaneous levies into a single tax known as the land-poll tax, which was more complete than the Ming system.

Industry and Trade Before the Opium War The mining of ores — gold, silver, copper, iron, tin, lead, mercury, cinnabar, realgar (red arsenic) and coal — made considerable progress. According to one report, there were ten or more mines in Guangxi Province, each employing about 10,000 men. In Yunnan there were forty-five mines. Some were government enterprises, and some were financed by the government and contracted out to merchants, others were private concerns. The salt industry was highly developed in Sichuan. In the porcelain works at Jingdezhen in Jiangxi, there was an elaborate division of labour. Tea-processing workshops in Guangdong Province employed up to 500 workers each. During the reign of Dao Guang there were 2,500 spinning and weaving shops in Guangdong, employing a total of 50,000 workers. The silks and satins of Jiangsu and Zhejiang, the brocades of Sichuan, the plain satin of Shanxi and the cotton cloth of Shandong and Henan were all celebrated handicraft products of the time. Capitalism, which had germinated under the Ming, experienced a further growth.

The salt merchants of Yangzhou and the money-houses of Shanxi were the most powerful elements in the business circles. The Shanxi money-houses are of special interest, for they possessed most of the characteristics of modern banking, handling remittances, accepting deposits, lending money and also collecting revenue on behalf of the government.

Foreign trade developed, and there was formal intercourse between China and tsarist Russia in 1655-60. The subsequent Treaty of Nerchinsk signed in 1689, and that of Kiachta, signed in 1727, delimited a boundary line in the middle and eastern parts of the border between the two countries and established regular commercial relations between them.

As for maritime trade, China continued her commercial relations with the Portuguese, Spaniards and Dutch. In 1685 the British opened a trading establishment (then called a "factory") in Guangzhou, and the East India Company began to extend its activities into China. In 1793 Lord Macartney arrived in China as a special envoy, seeking permission for British merchants to trade at the ports of Zhoushan, Ningbo and Tianjin. This was refused by the Qing emperor. The Qing government, being anxious to maintain its feudal rule intact, adopted a strict "closed-door" policy towards foreign trade, which was only permitted in the port of Guangzhou, and foreign traders were required to carry on business through the medium of a mere handful of merchants, known as the Co-hong (a kind of guild).

During the second half of the 18th century European capitalism sought to extend its commercial activities all over the world, and China, being a vast country with a large population and immense natural resources, was regarded as an ideal opening for this purpose. Foreign penetration of this potential market ultimately led to the outbreak of the Opium War in 1840, when the British aggressors used guns to force open the door of China. Foreign capitalism and the domestic feudal forces gradually entered into collusion to prevent the development of Chinese capitalism. This marked the beginning of a semi-colonial and semi-feudal society in China.

Culture in the Period Before the Opium War The philosophical school of Wang Shouren, the rise of which had coincided with the gradual disintegration of feudal society, and which had become the main ideological pillar in the later stage of feudalism, lost its hold with the coming of the Qing Dynasty. It is true that at the end of the Ming and the beginning of the Qing period there were still men who, like Huang Zongxi (1610-95), continued to disseminate the teachings of Wang Shouren, but that was the last faint echo of this school. Its opponents included Gu Yanwu (1613-82), who advocated the theories of Cheng Yi and Zhu Xi, and Wang Fuzhi (1619-92), who propounded materialist ideas. Wang Fuzhi was a great thinker, whose teachings closely approximated to those of early bourgeois philosophy.

During the reign of Emperor Kang Xi, Ferdinand Verbiest (from Belgium) and other Catholic missionaries spread Western scientific knowledge while helping the Chinese government revise history books, and Chinese scholars like Wang Xichan (1628-82) and Mei Wending (1633-1721) studied Western science.

During the reigns of Qian Long and Jia Qing, 1736-1820, many Chinese scholars were intimidated by the high-handed and repressive policy of the Qing rulers towards cultural ideas. Afraid to pursue utilitarian knowledge, as expounded by Huang Zongxi, Gu Yanwu, and Wang Fuzhi, they occupied themselves instead with textual research into ancient classical works with notable results.

In the early years of the Qing Dynasty the *kun qiang* (Kunshan drama) of the Ming was still in vogue, but after the reign of Qian Long, the Beijing opera gradually supplanted it as the main dramatic form. More novels were written in the vernacular, and well-known works of fiction like *A Dream of the Red Mansions* and *The Scholars* appeared.

MODERN PERIOD
(The Period of the Old Democratic Revolution)

I. THE OPIUM WARS

The popular rebellions and uprisings that took place in different parts of the country throughout the period from the closing years of the 18th century to the thirties of the 19th century indicated that the rule of the feudal landlord class, headed by the Qing aristocracy, was facing an increasingly grave crisis. It was at this period that marauding capitalist aggressors, exploiting the trade in opium, began to invade China and ultimately unleashed aggressive wars against it.

The Illicit Trade in Opium and the Ban on Opium Domestic handicraft industry was closely bound up with small-scale farming in the vast countryside of feudal China. This fact rendered it difficult for the British capitalists, who were anxious to dump their textiles abroad, to find a large market in China. The East India Company, which held a monopoly of British trade in China, was unwilling to pay for its silk and tea purchases in silver. For several decades, from the closing years of the 18th century, the East India Company, working hand in glove with Chinese officials in Guangdong, had sent large quantities of opium into China, either by bribery or by smuggling. This illicit trade was an enormous drain on China's wealth. American and other merchants also had a hand in these dirty transactions. It is estimated that more than thirty thousand chests of opium, valued at about twenty million silver dollars, were annually imported into China for a number of years. As the tremendous quantities of silver for its payment flowed out of the country, the financial burdens placed on the people became heavier and China's social production was seriously undermined. The financial crisis became so acute that the Qing government was forced to face it. The reactionary elements in the ruling circles were reluctant to impose a ban on the import of opium, but a section of the officials headed by Lin Zexu (1785-1850) demanded that the trade be strictly prohibited. In 1839 Emperor Dao Guang appointed Lin Zexu High Commissioner and sent him to Guangzhou to investigate matters and put an end to the opium trade. Backed by the power of the local people, Lin Zexu put up a determined struggle against the foreign opium traders and the law-breaking Chinese officials, gentry and merchants of Guangzhou. The British merchants, through their consul and representative, Captain Charles Elliot, handed over more than a million kilogrammes of opium, which was publicly burned at Humen (the Bogue) on June 3, 1839. In order to stamp out opium smuggling once for all, Lin Zexu issued a proclamation requiring every foreign ship entering the port to sign a bond testifying that there was no opium aboard.

The opium dealers were, however, determined to continue their iniquitous dealings and, acting on their behalf, Elliot requested the British government to send armed forces to China and to evacuate all British merchants from Guangzhou.

The War of 1840-42 The determined resistance organized by Lin Zexu prevented the British land and naval forces from landing in Guangzhou. In June 1840 the aggressors sailed north. Arriving at Xiamen (Amoy), they met with fierce resistance from the Chinese forces under Deng Tingzhen (1775-1846), Viceroy of Fujian and Zhejiang provinces. In July, the British took Dinghai, situated off the Zhejiang coast, and then proceeded to the mouth of the Haihe River near Tianjin. The Qing government, bent on seeking a compromise with the aggressors, removed both Lin and Deng, and sent Qi Shan, Viceroy of Zhili (now Hebei), to Guangzhou to sue for peace.

In 1841 Qi Shan demolished Guangzhou's defence works, agreed without consulting the central authorities to let the British occupy Xianggang (Hongkong) and indemnify the British merchants for their losses of opium. Emperor Dao Guang, however, refused to ratify these humiliating peace terms. He dismissed Qi Shan and declared war on Britain. On February 25, the British forces attacked Humen. Admiral Guan Tianpei put up a bitter resistance. His four hundred men defending the forts fought resolutely. They were all killed in action and Guan Tianpei was with them. The British warships entered Humen.

Three months later, Yi Shan, a general of the Qing court, signed an armistice with the British aggressors and paid them six million silver dollars as an indemnity for their non-entry into the city of Guangzhou.

The atrocities committed by the British aggressive forces and the shameful betrayal of the country by the officials of the Qing court aroused indignation among the masses of people. Tens of thousands of people rallied at

Sanyuanli, in the northwest of the city of Guangzhou, where they enrolled under the banner of the *Ping Ying Tuan* (Corps for Quelling the British Invaders). On May 30, this force succeeded in surrounding a body of over a thousand British troops. Other anti-British organizations of the people also rose in Guangdong Province, and by their heroic defence prevented the aggressors from committing further outrages there. These were the earliest actions taken by the Chinese people against foreign aggressors.

Within one year since August 1841, the British aggressive forces continued to harass the coastal areas of southeastern China, wrought great havoc in Zhejiang and Jiangsu provinces, and pressed right up to the wall of Nanjing. All along their paths they encountered armed resistance organized by the Chinese people. There were also government officials and commanders who had distinguished themselves by their patriotic deeds to their motherland; Yu Qian, Viceroy of Jiangsu, Anhui and Jiangxi, gave his life in the defence of Zhenhai in Zhejiang. General Chen Huacheng held the Wusong forts to the last. However, owing to the demoralization of the Qing forces, particularly of the Bannermen, and to the incompetence of the commanders, the resistance was not sufficiently strong to withstand foreign aggression. The ruling clique, with Emperor Dao Guang at its head, finally ceased all resistance and ignominiously bowed to the aggressors.

The Treaties of Nanking, Wanghia and Whampoa Under the Treaty of Nanking, signed on August 29, 1842, Hongkong came under British occupation, China was forced to pay an indemnity of 21,000,000 silver dollars, and the five ports of Guangzhou, Xiamen, Fuzhou, Ningbo and Shanghai were opened to foreign trade. The treaty further stipulated that the tariff rates on Chinese imports and exports must be jointly agreed upon by China and Britain. These provisions, which began to breach China's customs autonomy, together with the general regulations issued in 1843 governing the opening of the five ports and the granting of consular jurisdiction and special privileges covered by other documents, seriously impaired China's national sovereignty. Britain and other countries which later concluded similar treaties with China demanded and won from it the unilateral "most-favoured-nation treatment". The Chinese people were thus brought under the heel of aggressive capitalist powers.

The United States and then France came in the wake of Britain, both exacting further rights and privileges from China. The United States, which had played the role of accomplice in British military aggression against China, forced the Qing government to sign the Treaty of Wanghia in 1844. This wrested from China the right to engage in coastal trade and laid down more detailed stipulations concerning the exercise of consular jurisdiction. France used a number of warships to back up the spreading of the Catholic faith, making missionaries the tools of its aggression. The Sino-French Treaty of Whampoa was a copy of the Sino-British and Sino-American treaties. In addition to the provisions laid down in the treaty, the Qing court lifted the ban on the open practice of Roman Catholicism in China.

The Heroic Resistance of the Chinese People After the conclusion of the Treaty of Nanking, the people of Guangzhou refused to recognize the right of the foreigners to enter that city. Similar resistance was shown by the people of Fuzhou, but there the British consul was eventually allowed to enter the city on condition that the British flag was not to be flown at the British consulate. The people of Guangzhou, however, organized the *Sheng Ping She Xue* (Peace Society) and other mass armed organizations for the purpose of combating British aggression and uncompromisingly continued their struggle against the British and the capitulationist mandarins. They thereby made it impossible for the British to gain entry into the city for more than ten years. In 1845, the *Sheng Ping She Xue* launched a movement for the removal of the Guangzhou prefect and in 1849 it staged a demonstration against the presence of British gunboats in the port. These actions were crowned with success. The membership of the society grew from tens of thousands to hundreds of thousands. This patriotic force naturally incurred the hatred of the feudal ruling class. In 1855, during the period of the Taiping Revolution, Ye Mingchen, Viceroy of Guangdong and Guangxi, put 75,000 members of the society to death.

The Extension of Foreign Aggressive Designs After the signing of the Treaty of Nanking, the handicraft trades in many of the rural districts were adversely affected by the import of foreign manufactured goods and began to decline. But British manufactured goods, mainly textiles, were still unable to obtain a large market, and for more than ten years this trade made very little headway. Chinese exports of tea and silk on the other hand continued to increase, with the result that China achieved a favourable balance of regular trade. At the same time the British smuggling of opium into China became more rampant, the opium imports in the year of 1850 exceeding fifty thousand chests.

British capitalists, however, continued to believe that China offered an unlimited market for Manchester textiles. They demanded the opening of additional ports in north China and along Changjiang and tried to extort other privileges in order to make it easier for them to dump their merchandise in the country. The bourgeois of the United States and France were also willing to take joint action with the British. From 1854 on, these three powers began to press the Qing government for a "revision of the treaties".

By this time tsarist Russia had begun its aggressive activities in northeast China. The Russian Minister Putiatin, who arrived in Tianjin in 1857 and proceeded to Shanghai the following year, demanded that Russia should be given the right to trade at various coastal ports. This demand was rejected by China. He then entered into league with the British, Americans and French in their joint aggression against China.

The War of 1856-60 The second Opium War broke out in October 1856, when the British, using "The *Arrow* Case" as a pretext, launched a military attack on Guangzhou. The truth about "The *Arrow* Case" is this: A group of Chinese officers had been ordered to arrest some people aboard the Chinese lighter *Arrow*. The British would not allow them to carry out their duty, alleging that the ship had been registered in Xianggang as a British vessel. The British registration licence had in fact expired, and there was no justification whatever for the assertion that the vessel was a British one. The British felt that there was no need to fear Chinese opposition, because the resistance movement of the Chinese people in Guangzhou had been severely weakened under the high-handed policy of Qing officials. However, the popular militia in Guangzhou was still able to put up a heroic fight and succeeded in repulsing the aggressive British forces. The reactionaries, who advocated a compromise with the aggressors, took further repressive measures against the militia and finally forced it to disband.

Shortly afterwards, France, under the pretext of the murder of a French Catholic father, Père Chapdelaine, who had illegally entered Guangxi, joined hands with Britain, and a combined force of French and British attacked Guangzhou in December 1857. The following year this combined force took Guangzhou, then turned northward, entered Dagu in April 1858 and occupied Tianjin in May. The Qing government, which was then heavily engaged in the suppression of the people's revolution of the Taiping Heavenly Kingdom, did not intend to resist the foreign aggressors. It immediately complied with their demands and signed the Sino-British, Sino-French, Sino-U.S. and Sino-Russian Treaties of Tientsin. These treaties, apart from indemnifying the British and French aggressors for their expenditure on the war, provided for the opening of the six coastal cities of Nuzhuang, Dengzhou, Tainan, Danshui, Chaozhou, and Qiongzhou, and four cities along the Changjiang River, Hankou, Jiujiang, Nanjing and Zhenjiang as trading ports. The government also accepted the demand for the employment of foreigners in the customs service, gave permission for foreigners to travel and carry on trade in the interior, foreign missionaries to propagate their religion freely, and foreign warships to enter various Chinese ports. In 1859 further negotiations took place in Shanghai and as a result the opium trade was legalized, the tariff rate for all imports and exports was fixed at five per cent *ad valorem* (silk and tea for export and opium for import excluded) and the transit duty was fixed at two and a half per cent.

The British and French ministers accompanied by armed forces proceeded to Beijing in 1859 to effect an exchange of ratifications of the Treaties of Tientsin. Instead of following the route prescribed by the Qing government, they insisted on forcing their way into Dagu. They were repulsed by the Chinese defending forces despite the assistance of American warships. In August 1860 a large force of British and French troops succeeded in effecting a landing, took Dagu and Tianjin and entered Beijing. They wantonly set fire to Yuan Ming Yuan (the old Summer Palace) and carried out innumerable acts of looting and vandalism. Emperor Xian Feng, who had fled to Rehe, instructed his brother, Prince Gong, to negotiate with the invaders. The prince agreed to pay an indemnity of more than sixteen million taels on the security of the customs, granted foreign envoys the right to reside in Beijing, opened Tianjin as a treaty port and gave permission to Britain and France to hire Chinese labourers for work in their colonies — practically selling out the Chinese to work as slaves for foreign aggressors. A portion of Kowloon township was ceded to Britain and Catholic priests were granted additional facilities to carry on their activities in China. The Qing government shamelessly acceded to all the rapacious demands of these foreign pirates, in order to secure in exchange their co-operation in the suppression of the people's revolution.

Following the two Opium Wars the reactionary forces of Chinese feudalism began to unite more and more with the foreign capitalist robbers, in the effort of strangling the Chinese people's revolutionary movement, holding back China's advance from feudalism to capitalism, and dragging it deeply into the misery of semi-colonial and semi-feudal existence.

II. THE TAIPING REVOLUTION

The Taiping Revolution and Its Initial Successes The invasion of China by foreign capitalism in the forties of the nineteenth century and the increasing import of opium combined to subject the Chinese peasantry to greater exploitation than ever before. To meet the enormous cost of the war reparations, the Qing ruling class laid additional burdens on them. Poverty, bankruptcy and the menace of death from starvation forced the desperate peasants to rise up in resistance. Under the increased burden of taxation the petty traders and craftsmen also joined secret societies in large numbers. Moreover, workers like porters and boatmen, whose livelihood was seriously threatened because of the changes in the routes of transport caused by the opening of additional ports, nursed a deep hatred of foreign aggression and took an active part in the revolution. The anti-Qing uprisings of the people in various parts of the country, which had taken firm root, broke out afresh and coalesced in the nation-wide Taiping Revolution. The uprisings among the ethnic minorities which occurred during the same period were also influenced, to some extent, by the Taiping Revolution.

The leader of the Taiping Uprising, a poor school teacher named Hong Xiuquan (1814-64), came of a peasant family. A native of Huaxian County in Guangdong

Province, he became acquainted with the anti-Qing ideas spread by the *Tian Di Hui* (Heaven and Earth Society), and subsequently acquired some of the teachings of Christianity from foreign missionaries. In 1843 he founded the *Bai Shang Di Hui,* a society for the worship of God, which aroused and rallied the people to revolution in the names of God and Christ. Making use of the simple tenets of Christianity, Hong taught and spread theories of political and economic equality and also of the equality of the sexes. He won many followers among the poor peasants. Individual landlords and merchants who had been oppressed by politically powerful landlords also joined Hong's organization. From 1847 onwards, he and another revolutionary leader, Feng Yunshan (1821-52), led their followers in a series of fierce struggles against the armed forces of landlords. Later Hong formed a leadership consisting of seven men and on January 11, 1851, at Jintian Village in Guiping County, Guangxi Province, started the uprising and inaugurated the state which he named "The Taiping Heavenly Kingdom".

The Taipings, quickly breaking through the cordon of government troops by which they were surrounded, attacked Guilin and Changsha, took Yuezhou, Wuchang and Hankou, and then advanced eastward down the Changjiang River. In less than three years they fought their way from Guangxi to Nanjing. The Taiping force quickly grew from ten thousand men to an army of more than a million. They directed their main efforts to the removal of the officials, powerful gentry, landlords, and usurers. As they advanced, they burned land tax registers, land deeds and loan contracts. They confiscated property and distributed it to the poor. For this reason, large numbers of peasants, along their line of march, joined the Taiping army, and the peasants eventually became the main force of the revolutionary rank and file. Handicraftsmen and poor people of the cities who had belonged to the various secret anti-Qing societies also joined the Taiping army.

The Taipings set up a government in Nanjing in 1853. The first thing it did was to institute the Land System of the Heavenly Dynasty. This was a flat contradiction to the system of landlord ownership and put forward the principle that every peasant was entitled to sufficient land to provide him with a livelihood. The views of the Taipings on the land question, whilst an expression of the thoroughgoing anti-feudal character of their regime, embodied the idea of an absolutely equitable distribution of land and on this basis, a common ownership of property. This, of course, could not be realized. In the cities and towns, the Taipings encouraged the establishment of artisans' workshops for various trades, thereby raising the efficiency of production. They adopted a liberal trade policy and imposed light taxes which were collected in a simple manner. As a result trade flourished and large quantities of silk and tea were exported from the areas under their control. Trade in opium was completely banned.

The Failure of the Taiping Heavenly Kingdom After the capture of Nanjing, the Taipings committed a strategic blunder. They did not launch an all-out attack on Beijing, the centre of feudal rule; nor did they occupy Shanghai, the stronghold of foreign capitalism. In 1853 they directed Lin Fengxiang (?-1855) and Li Kaifang (1824-55) to lead an expedition into the northern part of the country. This expedition, after fighting its way through several provinces, reached the outskirts of Tianjin but failed to take the city because of lack of reinforcements. When leading his troops up Changjiang, the Taiping military leader Shi Dakai (1831-63) encountered the resistance of the leader of the armed forces of the landlords, Zeng Guofan (1811-72). The Qing troops had become demoralized by this time but Zeng Guofan did all he could to mobilize the strength of all the middle and small landlords in the interests of the Qing rulers. He was a ruthless traitor and killer, and his "Hunanese troops" became the most deadly opponents of the Taiping army.

By 1856, as a result of internal dissension, a serious split had developed among the Taiping leaders. One of their members, Wei Changhui (?-1856), who came of a landlord and wealthy merchant family, killed the brilliant military leader, Yang Xiuqing, a man of poor peasant origin, and slaughtered several thousand of his men. Wei himself was killed shortly afterwards. Another Taiping military leader, Shi Dakai, also of landlord origin, detached his command from the main body of the Taiping army and carried on isolated campaigns. The forces of the Taiping Revolution were thus greatly weakened and lost their military initiative. During the remaining years of the Taiping struggle the main responsibility for leadership rested on the shoulders of two talented young commanders of poor peasant origin, Li Xiucheng (1823-64) and Cheng Yucheng (1837-62).

After the end of the second Opium War the predatory demands of the capitalist powers from China had been temporarily satiated. In order to help the Qing court maintain power and thus preserve their own vested interests, they shifted the weight of their armed might against the Taiping army. In 1860 F. T. Ward, an American mercenary, built up an armed force which he recruited from among the foreign riff-raff in Shanghai and this he used, in co-ordination with the Qing forces, to attack and plunder the Taiping cities and towns. This mercenary force, the so-called "Ever-Victorious Army", had little real fighting power and was repeatedly defeated by the Taiping forces commanded by Li Xiucheng. Early in 1863 Li Hongzhang (1822-1901), an important commander of the Qing court, came to agreement with the British military authorities on the reorganization of the "Ever-Victorious Army". The agreement permitted British officers and men in active service to join it. Shortly afterwards the Qing government gave the British officer C. G. Gordon a commission and placed him in command of the "Ever-Victorious Army" under the direction of Li Hongzhang. Despicable and vicious methods were used by these two in order to induce certain wavering elements in the Taiping garrison at Suzhou to surrender the city to the Qing forces. The Qing forces, including the so-called "Ever-Victorious Army", entered the city in December 1863. Li Hongzhang and his troops perpetrated a wanton massacre of the people and a wholesale looting of the city.

French military and naval forces in China were meanwhile assisting another Qing commander, Zuo Zongtang (1812-85), in operations against the Taipings in Zhejiang Province. The forces of reaction and aggression grew stronger and stronger and it became impossible for the Taiping forces to resist any longer. On June 1, 1864, Hong Xiuquan died of an illness. On July 19 Nanjing fell. Not a single officer or man among the defenders surrendered. Many defied death by trying to break through the besiegers' lines, others sought death in blazing buildings. Li Xiucheng was taken prisoner and killed by Zeng Guofan.

Although it was purely a peasant uprising, the Taiping Revolution took on the purpose of opposing both feudalism and foreign capitalist aggression. Millions of poor peasants and staunch revolutionary leaders fought and died for their own ideal of liberation, although they did not clearly comprehend its significance. They upheld the glorious tradition of the Chinese working masses, who never yield in the face of internal or external foes.

Without the leadership of a proletarian class, the failure of this purely peasant war, pitted against such a powerful enemy, was inevitable. Nevertheless failure did not lessen the significance of the Taiping Revolution as a great dynamic movement which shook the Qing rule and shattered the capitalist powers' day-dream of a subjugated China.

The Uprisings of the Nian Forces and Various Ethnic Minorities The Nian forces, which operated in close co-operation with the Taipings, formed the backbone of the peasant revolution in north China. Early in the 1850s the Nian forces staged armed uprisings in Anhui and Henan. Between 1856 and 1860 they fought in co-ordination with the Taiping army and scored numerous successes, but these two revolutionary forces failed to unite and co-operate more closely. The Nian forces suffered from an absence of strict organizational discipline and were rendered less effective by internal strife. After the failure of the Taiping Revolution the Qing government devoted all its efforts to the suppression of the Nian forces, which were finally eliminated in 1868.

The Qing government had always acted in a most reactionary way towards the ethnic minorities. Like the Han people, the ethnic minorities waged constant and determined resistance against the Qing court and refused to submit to its rule. The Taiping Revolution had both a direct and an indirect influence on these peoples and stimulated them to rise up in large-scale armed resistance. Of these uprisings those of the Miao and the Hui peoples were the most important.

During the 1850s the Miao people in the province of Guizhou engaged in uprisings which continued for nearly twenty years (1854-72). At one time they established contact with the forces led by one of the Taiping leaders, Shi Dakai. The reactionaries committed the utmost cruelties in the suppression of these uprisings, and wiped out large numbers of the population. They killed a million people, but did not succeed in suppressing the Miaos.

Various ethnic minorities in Yunnan Province also defied the oppression of the Qing court. In 1855 the Hui people in different parts of the province rose in rebellion. The uprising at Yongchang in western Yunnan quickly assumed the proportions of a big movement. The Muslim Du Wenxiu gained the leadership during the course of the uprising, and as the various nationalities rallied under one common standard for the overthrow of Qing rule, the uprising rapidly spread all over the province. In 1867 Du dispatched a force of 200,000 men to attack Kunming. By the end of 1869 he had lost the greater part of his force in the vicinity of that city and was compelled to resort to defensive tactics. In 1873, the city of Dali which he was occupying fell and he poisoned himself. Following this defeat, many people of various nationalities in Yunnan were slaughtered by the Qing forces.

Between 1861 and 1863 the Hui people of Shaanxi and Gansu rose in response to the call of the Taiping Revolution. After the defeat of the Taiping forces, the Qing court sent a formidable army there under the command of the notorious warlord and butcher, Zuo Zongtang. In 1869 Zuo drove the insurgents into northern Shaanxi, encircled and massacred them, and then advanced into Gansu with his men. After five years of fighting all the bases of the Hui insurgents were destroyed. Those Huis who sought refuge in Suzhou, Gansu, their last stronghold, were nearly all wiped out in 1873.

In 1864 the ethnic minorities of Xinjiang also launched struggles against the barbarous oppression of the Qing court. These struggles continued until 1876, when Zuo Zongtang led large forces into Xinjiang and carried out further repressive measures there. In destroying the reactionary feudal forces of the British-fostered local despot Yakub Beg in south Xinjiang, he saved the people of Xinjiang from imperialist enslavement. In this respect Zuo Zongtang did something favourable for the Chinese people.

All these uprisings of the ethnic minorities were closely connected with those of the Taiping and the Nian forces. The movement of resistance against the rule of the Qing court was carried on by various nationalities all over the country. The barbarous massacres perpetrated by the reactionaries could not stifle the indignation and hatred of the people. On the contrary, they steeled their will to resist.

III. THE POSITION OF CHINA IN THE EIGHTH AND NINTH DECADES OF THE 19TH CENTURY

The Reduction of China to a Semi-Colony After its defeat in the Opium Wars, China began to acquire the characteristics of a semi-colonial country. As the reactionary forces increasingly joined hands with foreign reaction in order to suppress the ever-growing resistance of the Chinese people, the semi-colonization of the country was accelerated. The Qing government was shaken to its very foundations by the Taiping Revolution. The rulers, fighting for their own survival, redoubled their oppression of the people and collaborated more with foreign capitalist-imperialists. The feudal regime headed by Empress Dowager Ci Xi depended upon the assistance of the Hunan warlord clique, led by Zeng Guofan, and the Anhui warlord clique, led by Li Hongzhang, for survival. For more than twenty years, from 1870 onwards, Li Hongzhang controlled the modernized Beiyang (northern) naval and land forces and carried out repressive actions against the people.

In the 1880s China's agricultural production began to recover from the effects of the prolonged years of war, which had wrought havoc in the countryside. The landlord class, however, continued its old policy of land concentration. Consequently, the standard of living of the common people fell. In order to meet ever-increasing financial deficits, the decadent, decrepit Qing court imposed new burdens on the peasants, small traders and petty handicraft workers. These took various forms, such as additional taxes, inland transit tax and forced levies. At the same time foreign capitalists, taking advantage of the nominal 5 per cent *ad valorem* import duty and the 2.5 per cent transit duty, imported large quantities of low-priced yarns, cotton goods, kerosene and tobacco. This steadily destroyed the important subsidiary production of rural communities and forced the peasants to sell their agricultural produce at low prices in exchange for expensive imported articles. The import of these foreign goods and machine-made articles also undermined the handicraft production of some goods in the cities and towns. From 1864 to 1894, the total value of China's import and export trade increased from 100 million to 300 million Haiguan (customs) taels. The main imports were opium and manufactured goods. Tea, silk, cotton and other raw materials were the main exports. Foreign ships monopolized the coastal and river-carrying trade. A foreign inspector-general controlled the customs administration and the policing of the seacoast. Foreign banks such as the British Hongkong and Shanghai Banking Corporation and the Chartered Bank of India, Australia and China dominated the banking and finance of China. Feudal exploitation and foreign economic servitude weighed upon the Chinese people like two giant mountains.

The "Westernization" Movement Among the Feudal Bureaucrats and Early Beginnings of Modern Industrial Capitalism in China At this time a section of the warlords and mandarins advocated what they termed "Westernization". By this they meant that China should rely on the power of capitalist countries and make use of their technical skill in order to buttress up their tottering regime. The leading figures in this movement were the warlords of the Hunan and Anhui cliques. During the sixties and seventies the Hunan and Anhui warlords, raising the cry that China must make itself strong, established munition industries. These were financed by the government and managed by bureaucrats and compradors. Foreign technicians were employed and foreign machinery was purchased mainly for the manufacture of goods for war purposes. These enterprises were run on lines similar to those of the feudal government industries.

The leaders of the "Westernization" movement also made their way into the shipping and mining industries. One of the best-known enterprises of this type was the China Merchants Steamship Navigation Company, which was founded by Li Hongzhang in 1872 and financed by private as well as government capital. Although it had commercial stocks, the company was entirely under the control of feudal warlords and compradors, the private shareholders having no voice in the management of its affairs.

By the 1880s a type of so-called "government-supervised and merchant-managed" enterprise was very much in vogue. These were enterprises in which merchants provided the finance and government officials were responsible for the management. One of them was the Shanghai Cotton Textile Mill planned in 1882, which actually started production ten years later. Under the incompetent and corrupt management of the mandarins these enterprises often suffered heavy losses. Their credit with the public was thus forfeited with the result that no one wanted to continue investing money in them.

During the same decade some individual capitalists started small-scale metal works, paper mills, match factories and silk filatures in Guangdong, Shanghai, Wuhan, and other parts of the country. These enterprises were the first industries founded by Chinese national capital, but under the double pressure of foreign capitalism and domestic feudalism, they had little opportunity to develop. The officials in charge of "Westernization" controlled all the machinery, endeavoured to make industry their special preserve, and did all they could to prevent the formation and growth of a national bourgeoisie.

The social conditions that gave rise to the beginnings of industrial capitalism in China led some contemporary intellectuals to advocate bourgeois political reforms. For example, Zheng Guanying, a businessman with concerns in Shanghai and its vicinity, wrote a book entitled *Sheng Shi Wei Yan (Warnings Served in a Time of Peace and Prosperity).* In this he expressed the view that China should learn not only the industrial technique but also the politics of the Westerners. This, of course, meant bourgeois politics. Many members of the landed gentry of Zhejiang Province urged the establishment of a parliament. This demand reflected the reformist democratic views of the feudal landlords of the Zhejiang-Jiangsu area, who desired to transform themselves into the national bourgeoisie.

Intensification of Foreign Capitalist Encroachment on China's Frontiers The greed of the predatory foreign capitalists knew no bounds. The opening of the Suez Canal in 1869 shortened the route for trade and military transport between the European capitalist states and China. The resulting flood of imports led in 1873 to a deep business depression in Shanghai and other cities. At the same time the foreign capitalists were desperately searching for more markets for goods. Consequently each power began a series of new aggressive attacks on the borders of China, endeavouring to obtain a springboard from which to monopolize the market and resources of selected areas.

In addition to giving support to Japan in its invasion of Liuqiu, a vassal state of China, the United States collaborated with Japan in the aggression against the Chinese territory of Taiwan. In April 1874, C. W. Le Gendre, a retired American consul, and a number of regular officers of the United States army and navy, joined the Japanese generals Okuma and Saigo in directing the landing of Japanese forces at Langqiao on the southern tip of Taiwan. They were stubbornly resisted by the people of Taiwan and failed to advance. In 1879 former U.S. president U.S. Grant, as a mediator between China and Japan, requested that Liuqiu be divided up between the two. China rejected the demand. In 1881, however, Japan occupied the whole of Liuqiu.

Britain, having annexed Burma piecemeal, extended its aggressive influence into China's Yunnan Province. In 1876 it forced the Qing government to sign the Chefoo Convention under which Britain obtained facilities to extend its military and economic activities into Yunnan, Sichuan, Tibet, Qinghai and Gansu.

France was equally active in pursuing its aggressive penetration into Viet Nam, from where it attempted to proceed into Yunnan. The intensified French aggression led to the Sino-French War of 1883-85, in which the "Black Flag Army" under Liu Yongfu (1837-1916) was the mainstay of the resistance. Liu Yongfu was a former leader of a peasant uprising in Guangxi and was subsequently forced to withdraw to the Sino-Vietnamese border. Another veteran general Feng Zicai (1818-1903), then in his seventies, inflicted a heavy defeat on the aggressive French army at Zhennanguan (now Youyiguan)

Pass in March 1885. This victory led to the collapse of the French Cabinet. Nevertheless, Li Hongzhang, then in power, was strongly in favour of the immediate conclusion of hostilities and signed a humiliating treaty with France.

The Sino-French War demonstrated the fiasco of the "Westernization" advocated by the mandarins and warlords who had been building up the munition industries for over twenty years. This fiasco was to be made more glaring and explicit ten years later in the Sino-Japanese War of 1894.

IV. THE SINO-JAPANESE WAR AND THE CRISIS OF THE PARTITION OF CHINA BY IMPERIALIST POWERS

Japan's Designs on Korea and China Korea stood in the same relation to China "as the lip to the teeth". For two thousand years the peoples of the two countries had maintained close cultural and economic relations. When Korea was invaded by the Japanese army, led by Hideyoshi, in the latter part of the sixteenth century, the Koreans under Admiral Li Sun Sin, with the aid of Chinese reinforcements, repulsed the aggression. This further strengthened the unity of the two peoples.

During the 1870s, that is, after the Meiji Restoration of 1868 in Japan, capitalism, closely linked up with the feudal economy of that country, began to develop. Japan's plan of aggression, later revealed by Prime Minister Tanaka, envisaged a stage-by-stage invasion of China's Taiwan, Korea, northeast China, Mongolia and finally the whole of China and the whole world. Japan's invasion of Korea coincided with its attempt to seize Liuqiu and Taiwan. In 1875 a Japanese warship intruded into the waters off Kanghwa Island, and immediately afterwards Japan forced Korea to accede to its demand for the opening of commercial ports and for a Japanese survey of the Korean coast. The Qing government, instead of helping Korea resist Japanese aggression, secretly advised it to open trade relations with Britain, the United States, France and Germany. They hoped this would serve as a check to Japan, but Japanese aggression in Korea became more widespread with every passing day.

In 1882 there was a coup d'état among the ruling class of Korea. Japan took advantage of the occasion to send troops to Korea and, in 1884, captured the Korean royal palace. This time the Chinese soldiers fought alongside the Korean people and together they defeated the Japanese. The Qing government tried to play off tsarist Russia against Japan. Japan, however, relying on the support of the United States, continued to extend its influence into Korea.

The Sino-Japanese War of 1894-95 In 1894 the Korean people led by the Tonghak Society (Eastern Learning Society) rose in protest against feudal oppression and imperialist aggression. The Korean government appealed to the Qing government for aid, and Japan seized this opportunity to invade Korea. By the time the Chinese troops arrived in Korea the uprising was already over. The Qing government sent a note to the Japanese government, proposing that Chinese and Japanese troops be simultaneously withdrawn from the peninsula. The Japanese refused to evacuate Korea, seized the king and occupied all the strategic points leading to the Korean capital, Seoul. As a result of Japanese provocation, war broke out between China and Japan.

In the battles, many Chinese officers and men displayed great valour. Zuo Baogui (?-1894), a military officer, and Deng Shichang (?-1894), a naval officer, and their men courageously fought the enemy. Both officers sacrificed their lives in battle in 1894. The war party led by the Emperor Guang Xu (reigned 1875-1908) and the Minister of Finance Weng Tonghe (1830-1904) saw the war as a means of extending their influence and had no practical plans for carrying it to a successful conclusion. The capitulationists headed by Empress Dowager Ci Xi and Li Hongzhang, totally unprepared for war, merely tried to persuade Russia and Britain to serve as a check on the Japanese. The capitulationists gained the upper hand. This accelerated the defeat of China, with the result that the Japanese occupied Korea, the Liaodong Peninsula and Weihaiwei. In 1895 Japan forced the Qing government to sign the Treaty of Shimonoseki, whereby China: (1) accepted the cession of the Liaodong Peninsula, Taiwan and the Penghu Islands to Japan; (2) agreed to pay an indemnity of 200 million taels to Japan to cover its war costs; and (3) granted permission to Japanese nationals to set up and run industries in the treaty ports of China.

On hearing the news of the cession of Taiwan, people of various nationalities living on the island, rallying around Liu Yongfu, continued to fight the Japanese for another six months. The mainland people rendered warm support and assistance to their heroic brethren. The Qing government, however, blockaded Taiwan and prevented supplies from reaching the island, eventually making it impossible for the heroic people of Taiwan to continue their struggle. For the next fifty years, from 1895 to 1945, when Taiwan was formally restored to China, the island people kept up their struggle against Japanese rule and for the return of the island to the motherland.

As Japan's occupation of Korea and the Liaodong Peninsula was a hindrance to tsarist Russia's designs on northeast China, Russia secured the co-operation of Germany and France in forcing Japan to return the Liaodong Peninsula to China. Although Britain's policy was to support Japan against tsarist Russia, it was unwilling to see Japan obtain any territory on the Chinese mainland. It therefore adopted a neutral attitude towards the Russian move. In these circumstances Japan had no alternative but to return the Liaodong Peninsula to China. But it secured an additional indemnity of 30 million taels as compensation.

The Imperialist Powers' "Spheres of Influence" By the time of the Sino-Japanese War, world capitalism had already reached the stage of imperialism. Monopoly took the place of free competition and the export of capital assumed a special significance. The provisions of the Treaty of Shimonoseki signed after the Sino-Japanese war made it possible for all imperialists to freely set up their industries in China. From then onwards, export of finance capital to China became the principal form of aggression used by the powers against the country. In order to facilitate their own capital investments in China, the various imperialist powers began to cut up the country into what they called "spheres of influence". From 1895 onwards the powers engaged in a scramble for bases of operation, and the country was in grave danger of being partitioned by them.

In 1895 France demanded and obtained the two Yunnan districts of Mengwu and Wude and extended the Vietnamese railway to Yunnan and Guangxi. It also sought to secure the right to exploit mines in Yunnan and the two neighbouring provinces of Guangdong and Guangxi. In 1897 it extorted a declaration from the Qing government, which agreed that China would not lease Hainan Island or the opposite territory on the mainland to any other power. In 1898 France secured the "lease" of Guangzhouwan.

Britain, unwilling to see Yunnan, Guangdong and Guangxi become exclusively French spheres of influence, demanded the cession to Britain of Yerenshan in Yunnan, and the opening of Wuzhou and other cities on the Xijiang (West River) in Guangxi as "treaty ports". In 1898 it obtained the "lease" of Weihaiwei, Shandong, as a counterpoise to Russia. It also secured the lease of the Kowloon Peninsula, the various islands in the vicinity of Hongkong and the gulfs of Dapeng and Shenzhen as a counterpoise to France.

Germany forcibly secured the "lease" of the Bay of Jiaozhou in 1897 and built the Jiaozhou-Jinan Railway. It also obtained the right to open mines within thirty li[1] of the railway and together with Britain constructed the Tianjin-Pukou Railway.

At the time of the Second Opium War tsarist Russia, taking advantage of China's misfortune, seized large parts of Chinese territory, including areas north of the Heilongjiang River, east of the Wusuli River and also land along the borders of Xinjiang Province in the northwest, amounting to one and half million square kilome-

[1]A li = ½ kilometre or roughly ⅓ mile.

tres in all. In 1898 it obtained the "lease" of Lushun (Port Arthur) and Dalian (Dairen) and the right to build the Chinese Eastern Railway. It secured the right for the construction of the Beijing-Hankou and Zhengding-Taiyuan railways (Belgium acted on its behalf in the negotiation for the former). As a counteraction, Britain made a loan to the Qing government for the building of a railway outside the Great Wall. Anglo-Russian rivalry was at one time very much sharpened. In 1899 Britain and Russia reached an agreement about the spheres for railway construction, recognizing the Changjiang basin as belonging to Britain and the territory north of the Great Wall as belonging to Russia.

This was how the imperialist powers staked out their "spheres of influence" in China: Tsarist Russia claimed the territory north of the Great Wall; Great Britain, the Changjiang basin; Germany, Shandong; part of Yunnan, Guangdong and Guangxi provinces belonged to Great Britain and part to France; and Japan regarded Fujian as under its control. This was taken as a prelude to the gradual partitioning of the whole of China.

The United States, having no sphere of influence in China, proclaimed the so-called "Open Door Policy" in 1899. This was a policy under which the powers were required to throw open their leased territories and "spheres of influence" in China, to enable the United States to enjoy equal opportunities and privileges in the exploitation of China and its people. It was also a demand that China throw open the whole country to the investment of capital by the imperialist powers, so that it would eventually become their colony. Britain was the first to welcome this policy and the other imperialist powers followed suit. It was in this insidious way that the United States began aggressive activities aimed at its domination of China.

The Qing Government as the Servant of Foreign Imperialism One group of the mandarins and landlords, headed by Empress Dowager Ci Xi, pandered to their own love of pleasure and luxury by welcoming the import of foreign goods. At the same time this same group opposed everything that smacked of capitalism for China. This group constituted the die-hard party. Another section of the mandarins and landlords, with Li Hongzhang as their leader, served the imperialist powers as compradors (or agents) and were in favour of learning from the imperialists so that they could serve them better in expectation of greater reward. This group became known as the "Westernization" clique. There were many differences between the two groups but they had one thing in common: they were both loyal servants of the imperialist powers.

After the signing of the Treaty of Shimonoseki the imperialists invested large sums of money in the construction of industrial plants and railways and in the sinking of mines in China. This gave them a vital control of Chinese economy. Britain and tsarist Russia made political loans to China amounting to 370 million taels. As all these loans were made with the customs revenue as security, Britain and tsarist Russia secured the power to manipulate the finances of the Qing government.

Li Hongzhang was one of the most faithful executors of the wishes of the imperialist powers. He went to Russia in 1896 to attend the coronation of the tsar, afterwards visiting England, France, Germany and the United States. He accepted a bribe from tsarist Russia and signed a secret treaty which virtually amounted to the sell-out of northeast China to Russia. Two powerful viceroys, Zhang Zhidong (1837-1909) and Liu Kunyi (1830-1901), were bitter opponents of Li Hongzhang's pro-Russian policy. They served as agents for Britain, the United States, France, Germany and Japan, and disposed of many national rights and interests to those countries.

The imperialist gangsters, making full use of China's corrupt ruling classes, did whatever they pleased, plundering the country in a most despicable way. As Lenin said: "... the European governments have already started to partition China. However, they have not begun this partitioning openly, but stealthily, like thieves. They began to rob China as ghouls rob corpses...."[1] This grave state of affairs, while reducing the Chinese people to a life of bitter slavery, accelerated the development of a revolutionary situation in the country.

V. THE BOURGEOIS POLITICAL REFORM MOVEMENT OF 1898

The Rise of Bourgeois Ideas of Political Reform Beginning in the 1880s, under the stimulus of the Sino-Japanese War, bourgeois ideas of reform, which had gained ground especially in Shanghai and Guangdong, found concrete expression in a demand for political reform. In 1895 just before the signing of the Treaty of Shimonoseki, Kang Youwei (1858-1929), a scholar from Guangdong who had been waiting in Beijing for the imperial examination, submitted a memorial to Emperor Guang Xu,

---

[1] Lenin, *Collected Works*, Vol. 4, Foreign Languages Publishing House, Moscow, 1960, p. 374.

opposing the Treaty and formulating proposals for political reform. This he did jointly with 1,300 other scholars who had come to Beijing for the same examination. Thus the "reformist movement" began.

After the Sino-Japanese War, new portents began to appear on China's economic and social scene. The government-financed industries, hitherto controlled by the group of mandarins who advocated "Westernization", were obliged to give an outlet for the investment of private capital. The feudal and autocratic government and its mandarins had, for more than thirty years, tried to monopolize all machinery and industries and forbidden the development of private enterprises. China's defeat in the Sino-Japanese War betrayed the worthlessness of the government-operated modern munition industries and the so-called modernization of the army and navy. Since the Treaty permitted foreigners to freely set up industries in China, the Qing government was forced to give official recognition to private industrial enterprises. It openly ordered the various provincial authorities to encourage the development of the textile industry and in 1898 even encouraged private capital to open munition factories.

National capitalism began to develop after 1895, and new cotton textile mills sprang up in Shanghai, Ningbo, Wuxi, Suzhou, Hangzhou and Nantong. By 1897 there were thirty cotton mills and silk filatures in Jiangsu, Zhejiang and Hubei provinces. The opening of the Nantong Cotton Textile Mill in Jiangsu was a great event in the industrial history of China. These new industries found it very difficult, however, to keep going in face of the oppression and the competition of imperialist undertakings. Factories financed by foreign capitalists appeared in increasing numbers, and these enterprises, secure in their abundant capital resources and their special privileges granted by the unequal treaties, were able to overwhelm the Chinese industries. To make matters worse, the reactionary government continually signed away mining and railway rights, making it impossible for China to develop its own heavy industry and leaving light industry unprotected. There was a growing consciousness among the rising bourgeoisie that certain political reforms must be worked out if their position was to be safeguarded.

At the same time China's total defeat in the war of 1894-95, combined with the threatened partition of the country by the imperialist powers, roused a certain section of the intelligentsia to demand political reforms. These intellectuals, who were imbued with capitalist ideas, were aware that the position of China could not be improved simply by the purchase of machinery and arms from abroad. They hoped that through political reforms China would take the path of capitalism. Their views were in accord with the demands of the rising bourgeoisie.

The Failure of the 1898 Reform Movement The leading advocates of the reform movement at the time were Kang Youwei, Liang Qichao (1873-1928), Tan Sitong (1866-98) and Yan Fu (1853-1901), with Kang Youwei as their leader. Yan Fu introduced the theories of Western democracy into China, while Kang, Liang and Tan organized "societies" and published newspapers in different parts of the country to propagate their ideas of reform.

In November 1897, Germany seized Jiaozhou Bay. With this event China faced the grave peril of a partition of the empire. Reformists in all parts of the land called popular attention to the serious crisis facing the country and propagated the idea of political reforms. In 1898 Kang Youwei founded the "Society for National Salvation" in Beijing. He issued warnings about the danger of national extinction and demanded the immediate adoption of reforms in the government. Emperor Guang Xu accepted Kang Youwei's views and appointed him and a number of his followers to high official posts and allowed them easy access to the emperor himself. During the 103 days from June 11 to September 21, 1898, many imperial edicts and new laws were proclaimed. They included the abolition of the stereotyped writing of essay as a principal feature in the examination for official posts, the establishment of Westernized schools, the disbanding of the Green Banner troops, the discharge of redundant officials, the opening of modern banks, the development of mines, the building of railways, the promotion of various other industrial enterprises, and the encouragement of inventions and discoveries. They also included the publication of newspapers and the formation of academic societies, the setting up of a translation bureau for the purpose of introducing Western ideas into China, the drawing up of a national budget and the publication of government financial reports. These measures represented the demands of the bourgeoisie and marked a great advance on the system of feudal despotism.

Although the reformists succeeded in getting these new measures promulgated in the name of the emperor, the die-hards led by Empress Dowager Ci Xi continued to hold the military and political power of the country and opposed every kind of reform. The new measures failed to come into effect. As a result, the struggle between the new and the old factions became acute. Empress Dowager Ci Xi plotted a coup d'état to stop all reforms. The reformists hoped to avail themselves of the troops of the warlord Yuan Shikai to protect the reforms and defeat the die-hards. Yuan Shikai, however, sold the information to the die-hards and betrayed the reformists. Acting quickly, Ci Xi immediately caused the emperor to be seized and imprisoned. On September 21 she announced her resumption of the regency. Six of the reformists, including Tan Sitong, were murdered.

This movement placed all its hopes for reform on the prerogatives of Emperor Guang Xu, consequently it was only a very feeble and fragile reformist movement.

After the failure of the movement some of the reformists turned to the later emerging revolutionary group of the bourgeoisie. Others, led by Kang Youwei and Liang Qichao, clung to their reformist position, and in the guise of monarchist-liberals became stubborn opponents of the bourgeois revolutionary movement.

VI. THE YI HE TUAN PEASANT MOVEMENT AGAINST IMPERIALIST AGGRESSION

The Anti-Imperialist Movement of the People as Reflected in the Opposition to Foreign Missionaries Foreign aggression was intensified following the failure of the reform movement which had counted on royal power as its mainstay. The increased aggression, coupled with the increasingly difficult lot of the common people caused by the burden of taxation, led to the anti-imperialist movement of the Yi He Tuan (Boxers of Righteous Harmony) in the closing years of the nineteenth century.

This organization was mainly composed of the peasant masses of north China.

Spontaneous struggles of the lower social strata of the Chinese people against imperialism had continued ever since the failure of the Taiping Revolution. They generally took the form of opposition and resistance to missionaries and mission societies, sent to China by the aggressive foreign powers. Relying upon the special privileges extorted at the point of the bayonet from China by their governments, the missionaries penetrated into the interior of China and engaged in covert spying as well as in open activities designed to enslave the Chinese people. These foreign missionaries, particularly the Catholics, established churches and expropriated estates. Backed by the armed might of their imperialist governments, they threatened local Chinese officials, interfered with the government administration and law suits, and recruited scoundrels as "converts", using them to oppress the common people. All this fanned the indignation of the Chinese people.

The Yi He Tuan Movement The great struggle against imperialism which had been brewing among the people for a long time broke out in Shandong in 1899 and quickly took the form of a movement of broad proportions. At first it was led by a secret society known as the Yi He Tuan. Training in boxing was a special feature of this society's activities. Its members were principally peasants, handicraftsmen, transport workers and other low-paid workers. The organization also included a fair sprinkling of riff-raff and landlords who were victims of religious persecution. It was natural that such a movement, based on the peasantry, should also oppose feudal oppression. But as Shandong was at that time a victim of aggression by German imperialism, the struggle of the Yi He Tuan was at first directed against the foreign aggressors and the foreign missionaries, the representatives of the aggressive force with whom the Chinese people were in closest contact. The Qing officials of Shandong Province vainly attempted to put down the movement by force. Their action only served to accelerate its tempo.

The Qing rulers had now become so weak that they were unable to cope with events and could only view the rapid spread of the movement with alarm. Moreover, the people's rebellion was taking place in the immediate vicinity of the capital. As the Yi He Tuan was against foreign missionaries they decided to seize its leadership and use the movement for their own ends. The Yi He Tuan was legally recognized, and underlings of the officials and even some government officials themselves took part in the movement in order to gain control of the leadership from within. The composition of the leadership became very mixed and led to the adoption of a new slogan by the Yi He Tuan "Support the Dynasty and Exterminate the Foreigners". With the legalization of the Yi He Tuan the movement spread rapidly from Shandong to the neighbouring provinces and finally to such cities as Beijing and Tianjin. In the summer of 1900 the city of Beijing was almost completely dominated by the Yi He Tuan and there were open attacks on foreign churches and the legations of the imperialist powers.

The Combined Forces of the Imperialist Brigands Against China in 1900 The imperialist powers decided to dispatch their own troops to suppress the Chinese people's revolutionary movement. The combined forces of the eight powers, Britain, the United States, Russia, France, Germany, Japan, Italy and Austria advanced on Beijing by way of Dagu and Tianjin. Although the Yi He Tuan had only primitive weapons, it fought bravely against the foreign aggressors. Some of the officers and soldiers of the Qing army also took part in the fighting. The troops of the imperialist powers had superior equipment and indiscriminately killed civilians and burned villages in the course of their advance on Beijing. In August 1900 they marched like robbers into Beijing and sacked the whole city in search of "war booty". The outrages and atrocities — arson, looting, killing and raping — committed by these aggressive armies in and around Beijing, Tianjin, and Baoding have seldom been equalled in world history.

When the combined forces of the eight powers broke into Beijing the Qing court, led by Empress Dowager Ci Xi, fled to Xian. Before leaving it denounced the Yi He Tuan as "rioters" and made friendly overtures to the aggressive armies, requesting them to suppress the "rioters" on its behalf. The imperialists declared that they had not come to make war on China but had come to suppress the riots, put down the rebellion, and help the legitimate Chinese government to restore peace and order. Thus, hoodwinked at first by the feudal rulers, the members of the Yi He Tuan became the tragic victims of bloody slaughter by foreign imperialists working in league with the feudal forces at home.

The failure of the Yi He Tuan Movement demonstrated that without the leadership of an advanced class it was impossible for a peasant revolution to succeed. At the time of the movement, China had no independent proletarian class. The newly-born bourgeoisie was weak and lacking in determination, even the democratic revolutionaries among the bourgeoisie regarding the movement as a barbarous insurrection. Fighting by themselves, the peasant masses could not hope to succeed against the crafty and ferocious feudal ruling class plus the forces of imperialism. Nevertheless, the Yi He Tuan Movement revealed that among the Chinese peasants there was an immense potential force for the struggle against imperialism and feudalism. This force, which played an important role in subsequent Chinese history, compelled the imperialists to reconsider their policy towards China. The imperialists realized that if they partitioned China and brought it under their own direct control they would have to deal with countless struggles of the same kind. This caused them to decide to preserve a semblance of "Chinese independence", return the city of Beijing to the feudal Qing rulers, and act as wire-pullers behind the political scene of China.

The 1901 Treaty While the Yi He Tuan was waging fierce struggles against imperialism in the north, the viceroys and governors of the southern provinces adopted an attitude of "friendly co-operation" towards the imperialist powers. Because of the support received from the latter, they succeeded in suppressing the anti-imperialist movements of the people in central and south China. After the capture of Beijing by the joint forces of the eight imperialist powers, the Qing government appointed Li Hongzhang, then leader of the southern viceroys, to negotiate peace with them. In 1901 Li Hongzhang signed a protocol with eleven imperialist powers — Britain, the United States, Russia, Germany, Austria, France, Italy, Japan, Belgium, Spain and the Netherlands. Under its terms China had to pay an indemnity of 450 million taels, spread over a period of thirty-nine years. The total amount including principal and interest was more than 980 million taels. The Qing government was to be held responsible for the suppression of the Chinese people's anti-imperialist activities. Imperialist troops were to be stationed in Beijing and at all strategic points between Beijing, Tianjin and the Shanhaiguan Pass. The fort at Dagu, one of the most important in China's system of national defence, was to be demolished.

After the signing of the Protocol of 1901, the head of the Qing government, Empress Dowager Ci Xi, returned to Beijing from Xian, prepared to faithfully serve the imperialist powers and rule with their support. The imperialists felt that the Qing government was still a useful tool despite its corruption, and they could keep it in its place with the backing of their armed forces. The march of events was soon to upset this calculation.

VII. THE BOURGEOIS REVOLUTION OF 1911

The Chinese People Under the Yoke of Imperialist and Feudal Forces During the first decade of the 20th century the Qing government was completely subjected to the domination of the imperialist powers like a puppet. In addition to opening factories all over China the foreign intruders made further inroads into China's economy by grabbing its coal and iron resources. Britain, for example, seized and occupied the Kaiping (Kailan) mines, and Japan took possession of the coal mines in Fushun and the iron mines in Anshan. This made it impossible for China to develop its own heavy industry and to compete with them in such light industry as it had.

The foreign powers secured control of China's railways either through direct investment of capital or by the extension of loans at high rates of interest. The Chinese Eastern, Jiaozhou-Jinan and Yunnan-Viet Nam railways were examples of the first-mentioned, and the Shanghai-Hangzhou-Ningbo, Beijing-Hankou and Beijing-Shenyang railways examples of the latter.

The value of foreign investments in China before 1911 was U.S. $1,500,000,000. Foreign debts incurred by the Qing government amounted to U.S. $1,400,000,000, or £140,000,000 sterling, of which over U.S. $300,000,000 represented railway loans. Most of these loans carried a five per cent interest. The Qing rulers became the puppets of the foreign banks on the Shanghai bund. The annual excess of imports over exports in 1911 was more than 100 million Haiguan (customs) taels. All these burdens and many others fell heavily on the shoulders of the Chinese people.

Imported manufactured goods swamped the markets in cities and rural communities of China. Imports of cotton yarns went up sharply every year. Kerosene imports grew from less than 50 million gallons in 1891 to 150 million gallons in 1905. Imports of tobacco were valued at £660,000 sterling in 1905 alone. This was in addition to the processed tobacco turned out in China by the factories owned by the British and American Tobacco Company. Japanese raw silk forced sales of Chinese silk out of the overseas market. Exports of Chinese tea dropped from 260 million lbs. in 1886 to 180 million lbs. in 1905. The result was that depression in the Chinese silk and tea trade and decrease in production led to loss of means of livelihood for a big section of the people. China's other main exports at that time were mostly confined to agricultural products such as soya beans and bristles. The imperialist powers also had control of China's agricultural production and the semi-colonization of the country reached a point never before known in its history.

The tightened control over China's economic life, together with frequent encroachments on Chinese territory, provoked widespread resistance among the masses of the Chinese people. The Qing government, ever subservient to the imperialist powers, did everything in its power to suppress these patriotic activities of the people, holding that to be anti-imperialist was to be anti-Qing. In April 1903, the people of Shanghai demonstrated against tsarist Russia's refusal to withdraw its aggressive troops and its unreasonable demand for further encroachments on China's three northeastern provinces. In the same year, people in many parts of the country strongly denounced the plot of the governor of Guangxi to use French troops to repress the local people. Between May and November of 1905, the merchants and industrialists of Shanghai and six other ports boycotted U.S. goods. All these movements were ruthlessly suppressed by the Qing government, which at the same time tacitly assented to open and flagrant violations of Chinese territorial integrity by the intruders. For instance, when Britain invaded Tibet in 1904 and massacred 1,500 of the inhabitants of Lhasa, the Qing government not only failed to go to the aid of the Tibetans but subsequently connived at the drawing up of a humiliating secret treaty between the local rulers and the British. In the same year, when Japan and Russia were openly fighting in northeast China, the Qing government proclaimed the territory east of the Liaohe

River a war zone. These disgraceful acts fanned the indignation of the people of the whole country.

The Development of the Bourgeois-Democratic Movement

The bourgeois revolutionaries began to be more active. In 1905, a number of bourgeois-democratic revolutionary organizations, including the *Xing Zhong Hui* (Society for the Revival of China), which was led by Dr. Sun Yat-sen (1866-1925) since 1894, merged and formed in Tokyo the *Zhong Guo Ge Ming Tong Meng Hui* (Chinese Revolutionary League), also known as *Tong Meng Hui*, and elected Dr. Sun as its leader. The *Tong Meng Hui* adopted such slogans as "Drive Out the Manchus, Restore China, Establish a Republic, and Equalize Land Ownership." The *Tong Meng Hui* issued a manifesto in which it pointed out that "in addition to the expulsion of the Manchus and the restoration of China, the form of the state and the livelihood of the people must be changed, and although many complications are involved, the underlying spirit should be 'Liberty, Equality and Fraternity'. In the past there were heroes' revolutions; today we need a people's revolution".

Dr. Sun Yat-sen publicly announced the Three People's Principles — the Principle of Nationalism, the Principle of Democracy, and the Principle of the People's Livelihood. Under the Principle of Nationalism, though still lacking clear-cut ideas against imperialism, he advocated opposition to the Qing rule. Under the Principle of Democracy, he raised a call for the establishment of a democratic republic. Under the Principle of People's Livelihood, he propagated petty bourgeois Utopian ideas of socialism. Believing that China could avoid capitalism, Dr. Sun advocated the equalization of land ownership. He thought that by this means the peasantry would be emancipated from feudal oppression and at the same time the rise of capitalism could be "prevented". Lenin compared Dr. Sun's Principle of People's Livelihood with the *narodism* of Russia, and showed that in his programme the reactionary and visionary idea of preventing the development of capitalism was linked with the idea of a thorough-going democratic revolution. Lenin pointed out that the complete implementation of Dr. Sun Yat-sen's economic programme would actually clear the way for capitalism.[1]

During the first year of its existence the membership of the *Tong Meng Hui* grew to more than 10,000. The Qing government entered into collusion with the Japanese government for the persecution of its members. Nevertheless this combined force failed to halt the development of the revolution.

After 1905 the anti-Qing movement rose to full force. A succession of terrorist assassinations and abortive uprisings took place. What was more significant, an increasing number of intellectuals, peasant secret societies and soldiers of the Qing army joined the revolutionary movement with Dr. Sun Yat-sen at the head.

The Outbreak of the 1911 Revolution The Qing rulers, trying to save their tottering regime, announced a number of innovations which were calculated to mislead the people. They started a reform of the administrative machinery, legal and penal reform, adoption of a system of education based on European and American capitalist methods, unification of the national currency, promotion of the industry and commerce of the national bour-

---

[1] *Cf.*, Lenin, *Collected Works*, Vol. 18, fourth Russian edition, Moscow, pp. 143-49.

geoisie and encouragement of railway construction. They also promised to introduce a constitution and establish a parliament on the European model. These measures, however, failed to meet the demands of the people.

In May 1911 the Qing government, deferring to the wishes of its imperialist masters and ignoring popular opposition, issued a decree proclaiming the "nationalization" of all the railway trunk-lines in the country. The decree provided for the cash purchase of the railway shares by the government at 45 to 46 per cent of their original cost, the balance to be covered by the issue of bonds. Organized protest immediately broke out in Sichuan, Hunan, Guangdong and Hubei, for what the Qing government meant by "nationalization" was tantamount to placing the ownership of the Chinese railways in the hands of its foreign masters. In Sichuan an armed clash occurred between government troops and the petitioners. In the middle of September 1911, insurgent peasants laid siege to Chengdu, the provincial capital of Sichuan.

Events moved rapidly. On the night of October 10, 1911, an uprising broke out in Wuchang. It had been prepared with the utmost secrecy by two revolutionary organizations, *Wen Xue She* (The Literary Association) and *Gong Jin Hui* (The March-Together League), which had been active among the soldiers. Students and workers participated in the rising. The Qing viceroy fled. The revolutionaries quickly occupied the neighbouring cities of Hankou and Hanyang, and members of the *Tong Meng Hui*, scattered throughout the country, rose in support of the Wuchang revolutionary forces. The banner of revolution was thus unfurled over central China.

After the outbreak of the Wuchang Uprising, the revolutionaries found themselves short of trained troops. The men who had joined them were mostly labourers from the cities and rural areas with no fighting experience, and there had been no time to give them regular military training. Nevertheless, in the words of the representative of tsarist Russia in China, their courage made up for their technical shortcomings. It was courage that assured the success of the Wuchang Uprising.

The Crisis Lurking in the Rapid Success of the Wuchang Uprising The influence of the successful Wuchang Uprising spread rapidly to all parts of the country. Within a month revolutionary military governments were established in Hunan, Jiangxi, Shaanxi, Shanxi, Yunnan, Jiangsu, Zhejiang, Guizhou, Guangxi, Guangdong, Anhui, Fujian, Shandong, Fengtian and Sichuan, all declaring their "independence" of the Qing government. Delegates from these provincial governments met at Nanjing, proclaimed the founding of the Republic of China and elected Dr. Sun Yat-sen as President of the Provisional Government. On January 1, 1912 the Nanjing government was formed in opposition to the government in Beijing.

Although the Wuchang Uprising was swiftly successful because of the unpopularity of the Qing government among the people, it also revealed that a crisis was looming within the ranks of the revolution.

Because the Qing regime could no longer manage to maintain itself in power, the foreign imperialists were looking round for a tool more suited to serve their purpose and replacing the Qing court by it. A great number of monarchist-liberal elements and many mandarins and militarists now realized that "participation" in the revolution would be to their own interests. Some who had previously opposed the revolution now veered round and gave it nominal support, their object being to bring it quickly to a close and prevent the collapse of the old social rule and order.

The bourgeois-revolutionary leaders were incapable of mobilizing the real strength of China's democratic revolution — the strength of the peasantry, and of forming an alliance with the peasants and leading them forward. They were carried away by the rapid success. The bourgeois revolutionaries thus lost the leadership of the revolution during the course of its very successes. They were unable to defy the imperialists and to overcome the attack of the feudal forces, and eventually succumbed to the pressure of imperialist influence and brought the revolution to an end.

The Failure of the 1911 Revolution and Its Historical Significance The warlord Yuan Shikai, who had held the real military power behind the Qing government and had always enjoyed the favour of the imperialist powers, became the "hero" of the 1911 Revolution who usurped its fruits. He compelled the Qing court to abdicate in his favour and coerced the Nanjing government into handing its powers over to him and to "elect" him the first President of the Republic of China. In March 1912 Yuan Shikai declared himself President of the republic. This announcement signalled the defeat of the first bourgeois revolution.

Despite its failure, the bourgeois revolution of 1911 was of profound historical significance. In the first place, it overthrew the Qing Dynasty, a rule of nearly three hundred years and made the restoration of the more than 2,000-year-old feudal monarchical system impossible.

This was of great importance in the further awakening of the Chinese people.

International imperialism was upset by the disturbances which followed the China 1911 Revolution. It was only when Yuan Shikai assumed power that they felt reassured. The 1911 Revolution clearly revealed the weak and compromising character of the Chinese bourgeoisie.

VIII. CHINA BEFORE AND AFTER THE FIRST WORLD WAR

China's Plight Under the Twofold Oppression of Imperialists and Warlords The years from 1912 to 1919 constituted one of those periods of darkness and anarchy which have characterized the modern history of China.

Under the autocratic rule of Yuan Shikai the country continued to be governed by the big landlords and comprador bourgeoisie. Yuan Shikai flagrantly carried on the policy of selling out the country and, with the support of the imperialist powers, attempted to crown himself "Emperor". He failed to establish a monarchy and after his sudden death in 1916, political power fell into the hands of Yuan's successors — a group of military leaders known as the Beiyang warlords. When one of the various cliques, into which these warlords were divided, seized control of Beijing, it set up a so-called "Central Government". This "Central Government" became the prey of warlords, bureaucrats and various shameless politicians. The warlords of the different provinces maintained huge military establishments, each regarding himself as the "supreme authority" in his own region and fighting the others in internecine wars.

The various imperialist powers continued to freely exploit the Chinese people and impose their will on Chinese affairs by manipulating the so-called "Central Government" at Beijing and the "local governments" of the numerous smaller warlords. World War I forced the Western imperialist powers to relax their aggressive activities in China to some extent, but the Japanese imperialists took advantage of this opportunity to expand their influence in China. After the October Socialist Revolution in Russia, the warlords' regime in Beijing followed Japanese imperialism in its intervention against the Russian Revolution.

The defeat of the 1911 Revolution had forced the bourgeoisie of China to admit that the democratic republic which they had cherished was still-born. A large section of the bourgeoisie, however, were willing to throw in their lot with the feudal warlords in order to share in the booty. Another section, led by Dr. Sun Yat-sen, refused to compromise with the feudal warlords, but were at a loss to find a way to advance the revolution, not knowing where they could find the necessary strength for the salvation of China.

The workers, peasants and the petty bourgeoisie of the towns and cities continue to suffer and groan under the ruthless oppression of imperialism and feudalism. The intellectuals groped painfully in the dark for a way out. The tragedy of China during the previous eighty years, the failure of the 1911 Revolution, the great war of the imperialist powers, and finally the victory of the October Socialist Revolution in Russia — all had a profound effect on the Chinese intellectuals and the masses of the oppressed people.

Further Development of Chinese Capitalism During the First World War At this time new factors began to appear in the Chinese social order. They arose out of the development of Chinese capitalism.

Chinese capitalists seized opportunities arising out of this war to extend their activities, and industries owned by members of the national bourgeoisie made considerable headway. This was particularly true of the cotton spinning industry, which increased from 651,676 spindles in 1913 to 1,173,012 in 1919. During the same period, however, Japanese industrial enterprises in China also expanded and competed with the capital of the Chinese national bourgeoisie. After the war ended, Great Britain, the United States and other imperialist powers returned to the scene of their former aggression. Their pressure on the capital of the Chinese national bourgeoisie was too heavy to be borne. This state of affairs forced the national bourgeoisie to a struggle.

The most important new factor in the situation was the fact that the working class had grown in strength as a result of the development of national capitalism and of the expansion of the foreign-owned industrial enterprises. The number of workers had increased from less than one million in 1914 to about three million in 1919. Although the Chinese working class was still not politically conscious, it was already developed on the eve of the May 4th Movement in 1919. It had initiated many strikes, although as yet none of these had taken on a political character. It had already formed organizations of different types, though a party of its own or centralized trade union leadership was still absent. Under the triple oppression of feudalism, capitalism and imperialism, the Chinese working class had matured with a deep hatred of the reactionary forces. This meant that once the Chinese working class acquired leadership and became politically conscious, it would quickly develop into a force capable of independent action.

The emergence of these new factors in the dark years that followed the 1911 Revolution ushered in the dawn of a new era in Chinese history simultaneously with the advance of the world history as a whole.

IX. NEW LEARNING AND OLD LEARNING

Prior to the Opium Wars, the ruling class in the feudal society of China had had its own culture, known as the Old Learning. The bourgeois culture which was introduced from abroad after the Opium Wars came to be known as the New Learning. Supporters of the Old Learning were hostile to the New Learning and seriously hindered its dissemination and growth.

The New Learning embraced the social theories and natural science of the Western bourgeoisie. Progressive Chinese as represented by Hong Xiuquan, Kang Youwei, Yan Fu and Sun Yat-sen studied these social theories and wanted to apply them for the salvation of China. Important works representing the New Learning in the field of social theories included Hong Xiuquan's *Tian Chao Tian Mu Zhi Du* (*The Land System of the Heavenly Dynasty*) and the *Zi Zheng Xin Pian* (*A New Book on Government*) written by Hong Rengan; Kang Youwei's *Bian Fa Wan Yan Shu* (*Ten Thousand Words on Political Reform*) and *Da Tong Shu* (*The Book of Great Harmony*); Yan Fu's translations of Adam Smith's *The Wealth of Nations*, Montesquieu's *L'Esprit des Lois*,

Thomas Huxley's *Evolution and Ethics,* Herbert Spencer's *The Study of Sociology* and John Stuart Mill's *System of Logic*; Dr. Sun Yat-sen's *The Three People's Principles* and the writings of Tan Sitong and Liang Qichao.

All these authors advocated reformism, with the exception of Hong Xiuquan and Sun Yat-sen who expounded revolutionary theories. Although reformist writings were also denounced by the followers of the Old Learning, they nevertheless obtained a wide circulation among the intellectuals, to whom they were primarily addressed. The reformist writers propagated bourgeois culture and encouraged the intellectuals to challenge and combat feudal culture. In the combats they were, in the main, worsted. However, they gained some minor victories on some topical issues.

The Chinese people accumulated experience and learned from their failures, particularly that of the 1911 Revolution. The latter had demonstrated that the bourgeoisie and petty bourgeoisie could not obtain revolutionary victory for a semi-colonial country like China during the era of imperialism, and that bourgeois culture was no help in the struggle. This was a very important lesson, which demonstrated that the Chinese people's revolution must be led by the proletariat, and their culture must be the proletarian culture.

Throughout this period the study of natural science was more favoured than social science, a section of the feudal rulers having need of it. A translation department set up at the Jiangnan Arsenal in Shanghai translated many foreign books on mathematics, mechanics, electricity, chemistry, sound, light, steam, astronomy, geography, physiology, psychology, zoology, botany, medicine and cartography. Liang Qichao in his preface to the *Catalogue of Western Books* said:

> If China wants to become strong, it is of primary importance to translate as many Western books into Chinese as possible; if the student wants to accomplish anything, he must read as many Western books as possible.

This quotation shows the importance which people of the period attached to the study of the natural science.

Towards the closing years of the Qing Dynasty new schools of various grades were opened, and natural science became one of the compulsory subjects. More progressive intellectuals, dissatisfied with the level of the science then taught in Chinese schools, and cherishing an illusion of making China strong and independent through greater knowledge of natural science, went to other countries to seek more knowledge. A tremendous number of students went abroad for the same purpose, and many attained distinction in their chosen fields, but on their return had very little opportunity of putting their knowledge to practical use. Some became officials; others engaged in occupations which presented no opportunities for the application of their learning. Natural science in China remained weak and undeveloped, despite the fact that many Chinese had obtained scholastic honours in this field.

The policy of the feudal rulers was to "make Chinese learning the basis, and adopt Western learning for practical purposes". What they meant by "making Chinese learning the basis" was to preserve the Old Learning of feudal culture and exclude the New Learning of bourgeois culture. What they meant by the "adoption of

Western learning for practical purposes" was to endeavour to bolster up the feudal rule by making use of natural science.

The imperialist powers and the feudal rulers restricted the spread of the New Learning. The slogans of "Democracy and Science", issued by advanced petty-bourgeois and bourgeois intellectuals before the May 4th Movement of 1919, were a manifestation of the dissatisfaction with this pressure.

The literature and art imported from abroad constituted part of the New Learning, but the works in these two categories were immature, and received far less attention from the bourgeois intellectuals than social theories and natural science. Comparatively speaking, literature was the more influential. Lin Shu translated more than a hundred foreign novels.

Generally speaking, the intellectuals who preached the New Learning at this time were sincerely desirous of learning something useful from Western culture. Although their social theories still retained some poisonous traces of Chinese feudalism and even contained the slave ideology of imperialism, they were actuated by a desire to save China. In teaching natural science they were also animated by the desire to make China strong and independent. They had nothing in common with the group of slavish worshippers of Western culture led by Hu Shi. The desire to make China strong and independent accounted for the fact that when the people's revolution entered the stage of the New Democratic Revolution, the progressive elements of the school of New Learning gradually came to realize that serving the bourgeoisie offered no future for them and that the worship of Western bourgeois culture would yield no result. When they saw the ultimate goal and success of the New Democratic culture, one after another they voluntarily enrolled in the big army of New Democratic culture. During the difficult years of the revolution a relentless campaign was waged, with Lu Xun as the spearhead, against feudal culture and "foreign slave" culture, and the campaign was everywhere victorious.

CONTEMPORARY PERIOD
(The Period of the New Democratic Revolution)

I. THE BEGINNING OF THE NEW DEMOCRATIC REVOLUTION

The May 4th Movement, the Founding of the Communist Party of China and the First Revolutionary Civil War (May 1919 to July 1927)

The May 4th Movement Against Imperialism The First World War came to an end in November 1918. The Versailles "Peace Conference" convened in Paris by the victorious imperialist powers opened in January 1919. This was a conference called by the predatory imperialist powers for the purpose of dividing the spoils of war, for the dismemberment of the defeated countries and the redistribution of their colonies. The Peace Treaty signed at Versailles by the imperialist powers, however, decided that Japan should take over all the special "rights" previously seized by Germany in Shandong Province — including the occupation of Qingdao and the control of the mines located along the Jiaozhou-Jinan Railway line. This aroused the indignation of the Chinese people. On May 4, 1919, students in Beijing held a mass meeting at Tian An Men, raising the slogan: "Uphold Our Sovereignty, Punish the Traitors!" They proclaimed their determination to fight to the last man against Japanese occupation of China's territory and demanded the punishment of three pro-Japanese traitors in the feudal warlord government — Minister of Communications Cao Rulin; the Chinese Minister to Japan Zhang Zongxiang; and Director-General of the Currency Bureau Lu Zongyu. From Tian An Men the students marched to the residence of the traitor Cao Rulin and set fire to it. Zhang Zongxiang, who was found hiding in Cao's house, was given a sound thrashing. The just struggle of the students in Beijing won the sympathy of the people throughout the rest of the country. The students were the first to take action by organizing classroom strikes. On June 3, a mass meeting, attended by people of all walks of life, took place in Shanghai. It issued a call for a general strike throughout the country in support of the students. On June 5, seventy thousand workers in Shanghai, Tangshan and Changxindian downed tools in a political strike against imperialism. This was the first time that the modern Chinese working class had appeared on the political stage as a militant force and played the main role in the Chinese people's struggle against imperialism. Merchants and students in all parts of China also staged strikes. The May 4th Movement, as it came to be called, developed into a combined revolutionary movement of workers, students and merchants with a broad popular base opposing imperialism and bringing great pressure to bear on the feudal warlord government. In the face of this pressure the reactionary government was forced on June 28 to refuse to sign the Versailles Peace Treaty. The news of the Chinese people's determined struggle against imperialism aroused the interest of the whole world. This popular revolutionary movement of a new type demonstrated that the great Chinese people had experienced a new national awakening. Its forthright anti-imperialist and anti-feudal spirit opened a new chapter in the history of the Chinese democratic revolution.

The Influence of the October Socialist Revolution on China At the same time as this patriotic anti-imperialist movement was developing, the more advanced Chinese intellectuals launched a new cultural movement which was directed against feudal culture. This new movement aimed at the promotion of democracy, science and a literary revolution.

With the rapid development of Chinese national industry during World War I and the swift growth in power of the two new classes in Chinese society, the working class and the bourgeoisie, there came a flood of new ideas concerning democracy, freedom and liberation. Prior to the October Socialist Revolution in Russia, the new cultural movement in China had mainly confined itself to the dissemination of bourgeois democratic ideas. The October Socialist Revolution, together with the subsequent proletarian revolutions in different countries in Europe and the national liberation movements of the various countries in the East, had a profound impact on events in China. The victory of the revolution in Russia set an example to the Chinese people and showed them the road to their own liberation. The Soviet government's abrogation of all the unequal treaties which tsarist Russia had concluded with China inspired them and deepened their sympathy and support for the socialist revolution. With the victory of the October Revolution a flood of socialist ideas flowed into China. A number of Chinese revolutionary intellectuals, represented by Li Dazhao (one of the founders of the Communist Party of China, who was put to death by the warlord Zhang Zuolin in April 1927), Chen Duxiu (one of the founders of the Party who later became a liquidationist), Mao Zedong and Zhou Enlai hailed the victory of the October Revolution. They pledged their faith in communism and became the first Chinese intellectuals to arm themselves with the ideas of communism. The new cultural movement in China, after coming under the influence of the October Revolution, was primarily concerned with the dissemination of socialist ideas.

The new cultural movement gave momentum to the patriotic May 4th Movement against imperialism, which, in its turn, further stimulated the cultural movement. Large numbers of periodicals, books and newspapers were put into circulation, their avowed object being the introduction and dissemination of new ideas. Intellectuals who began to have some knowledge of communism constituted the left wing of the new cultural movement, and played a leading role in it and in the patriotic movement against imperialism. Their propaganda, coupled with their criticism of bourgeois reformist ideas, enabled Marxism-Leninism to make rapid headway in China and won over a large section of Chinese youth. In this way the May 4th Movement paved the way both ideologically and organizationally for the founding of the Communist Party of China.

The October Socialist Revolution and the May 4th Movement radically changed the course of Chinese history. The Chinese revolution became part of the world proletarian socialist revolution. The Chinese democratic revolution became a revolution led by the working class, and China passed from the era of the old democratic revolution into that of the new democratic revolution, which was ushered in by the May 4th Movement.

As Mao Zedong pointed out, "The May 4th Movement

came into being at the call of the world revolution, of the Russian revolution and of Lenin."[1] During the period between 1918 and 1920, Lenin on many occasions gave most important guidance to the solution of the national problem in the East. At the Second Congress of the Communist International held in 1920, Lenin presented a specific programme on national and colonial issues and explicitly laid down the basic policy which Communists should adopt in the national revolutionary movement. The directives of Lenin illuminated the road of the Chinese revolution and gave impetus to its development.

The Founding of the Communist Party of China and the Development of the Working-Class Movement After the May 4th Movement, the Chinese working-class movement advanced considerably. Some intellectuals influenced by communism began to associate themselves with the workers in Changxindian, Shanghai, Hunan and other places, helping them to organize trade unions, clubs and part-time schools. They started newspapers in Beijing, Shanghai and Guangzhou, explaining in popular language the ideas of communism to the workers. In this way Marxism-Leninism began to be gradually integrated with the working-class movement.

The first Marxist group was formed in Shanghai in the summer of 1920. The Chinese Socialist Youth League was inaugurated in August of the same year. At about the same time, Marxist groups and Socialist Youth Leagues were organized in Beijing, Hankou, Changsha, Guangzhou and Jinan, and among Chinese students studying in Paris and Tokyo.

---

[1] Mao Zedong, "On New Democracy", *Selected Works*, Foreign Languages Press, Beijing, 1975, Vol. II, p. 373.

A congress held in July 1921 in Shanghai, the centre of China's industry, marked the foundation of the Chinese Communist Party. There were thirteen delegates, representing over fifty members of Communist groups scattered in various places. Those present included Mao Zedong, Dong Biwu, Chen Tanqiu, He Shuheng and Wang Jinmei. The congress decided to establish a Chinese Communist Party after the pattern of the Russian Bolshevik Party. It adopted a constitution and elected a central committee. The Marxist revolutionary political party of the Chinese working class thus came into being. This was the most important and decisive event in the history of modern China. Despite its lack of size the Party, armed with the ideological weapon of Marxism-Leninism, was able to appear on the stage of history as organizer and leader of the revolution. It brought about profound changes in the character of the Chinese revolution and step by step led it towards victory. Two observers from the Communist International were present at the inaugurating congress.

The Chinese Communist Party correctly stated that its first main task was to organize the working-class movement in order that its strength could be mobilized and in order to ensure the close linking of the working-class movement and communism. The Communist Party set up the Chinese Trade Union Secretariat to provide open leadership for the working-class movement throughout the country. Under the triple exploitation and oppression of imperialism, feudalism and capitalism, the Chinese working class had been reduced to most miserable circumstances and robbed of all rights. It was, however, possessed of a strong and determined will for revolution and was in urgent need of liberation. Under the powerful leadership of its own party, the Chinese Communist Party, the fury of the working class burst like a volcano. The working class initiated the first upsurge of the Chinese labour movement in a struggle which lasted from January 1922 to February 1923. During those thirteen months several hundred members of the Chinese Communist Party and the Socialist Youth League (renamed the Chinese Communist Youth League in January 1925) launched and led more than one hundred strikes. The strikes involved more than 300,000 workers in the big cities, industrial and mining areas, and on the main railways and shipping lines of the country.

The strike wave began with a big walk-out of seamen in Hongkong in January 1922. They demanded wage increases and protested against oppression by the British imperialists. By the end of February, all the workers in Hongkong were on strike in support of the seamen. Workers in different parts of the country enthusiastically supported the Hongkong strikers. The strike ended early in March, with a complete victory for the seamen. Its success had the effect of greatly raising the militancy of the workers throughout the country. In May of the same year, the First National Labour Congress was convened in Guangzhou. Under the leadership of the Chinese Communist Party, the congress played an important role in bringing about the unified leadership of the working-class movement and promoting the struggle of the working class.

The Communist Party and the working class were greatly in need of a militant programme which would serve as a clear-cut target for their struggles and which would win the approval of all sections of the people. The Party convened its Second National Congress in

Shanghai in July 1922 to map out such a programme. Twelve delegates, including Chen Duxiu, Deng Zhongxia, Cai Hesen and Xiang Jingyu, representing 123 members, attended. The congress adopted a manifesto in which it set forth its basic programme for the Chinese revolution. The manifesto declared that the Party's maximum programme was the realization of the communist system in China. It worked out a detailed minimum programme for the Party — the basic programme for the attainment of the democratic revolution in China. The manifesto pointed out:

> It is capitalism-imperialism and the feudal forces of warlords and bureaucrats that are inflicting the greatest hardships on the Chinese people (whether they be bourgeois, workers or peasants), and for this reason the democratic revolutionary movement against these two forces is one full of significance.

The manifesto sounded the call for the establishment of a democratic united front and proposed a concrete programme for it. It defined the immediate basic tasks of the Chinese people as follows: "to eliminate civil strife, overthrow the warlords and establish internal peace; to overthrow the oppression of international imperialism and achieve the complete independence of the Chinese nation; to unify the whole of China (the three northeastern provinces included) into a genuine democratic republic."

The congress issued a militant call to the people of the whole country, urging them to struggle against imperialism and feudalism. It was the first of its kind in the history of China. From then on the Chinese people embarked on a determined and vigorous revolutionary struggle for their emancipation. The congress also adopted a resolution in favour of joining the Communist International.

The congress gave fresh impetus to the strike movement, and shortly afterwards there was a succession of strikes in Shanghai, Wuhan, Hunan and Guangdong, as well as a new wave of strikes among the railway, mining and shipping workers. The most important of these strikes were the strike of the miners at Anyuan Colliery in Pingxiang, Jiangxi Province, and those of the workers on the Zhuzhou-Pingxiang Railway. They took place in September 1922, and twenty thousand workers were involved. These strikes were followed in October by a stoppage of work by forty thousand Kailuan coal miners. Most of the strikes ended in victories for the workers.

When the imperialists and the feudal warlords saw that the strike movement was spreading and threatening to engulf the whole country, they joined forces and tried to put a stop to it by armed repression. On February 7, 1923 many workers on the Beijing-Hankou Railway were savagely slaughtered.

A general strike of the Beijing-Hankou Railway workers had developed out of their fight for the right to form a general trade union. On February 1, 1923 a number of delegates from trade union groups at the various stations met in Zhengzhou to inaugurate the General Trade Union of the Beijing-Hankou Railway. The warlord Wu Peifu sent a body of troops and armed police to the scene and broke up the meeting. Three days later, at noon on the fourth day of February, the workers all along the line stopped work in protest against this action. Their slogans were: "Fight for Freedom!" and "Fight for Human Rights!" On February 7, at the instigation of the imperialists, the military authorities ordered their troops to attack the strikers. At Jiangan, in Hankou, a number of workers were killed. On the same day similar atrocities took place at Changxindian and at Zhengzhou. These incidents came to be known in the history of the Chinese labour movement as the "February 7th Massacre". On that day, about forty workers were killed, over three hundred were wounded, forty were arrested. The headquarters of all the trade unions along the railway track were either wrecked or closed down. Among the martyrs were Lin Xiangqian and Shi Yang, both members of the Communist Party.

The Beijing-Hankou Railway Strike was the biggest and last of that period, and following this there was a temporary ebb in the tide of the working-class movement.

The first upsurge of the Chinese labour movement and the February 7th strike demonstrated the great strength of the working class which, along with the Communist Party, began to enjoy a much greater prestige politically throughout the country. The news of the strike movement spread among workers in other countries, enabling them to see the power of the Chinese working class.

The February 7th Incident raised new problems for the Chinese working class and the Communist Party. It showed that the working class could not depend upon itself alone to win the fight against its enemies. In the fight against the common enemy, the working class must form a revolutionary united front with every class capable of working for the revolution, and the revolutionary people must arm themselves to deal with armed counter-revolution.

Following the February 7th Movement, the Chinese

Communist Party took upon itself the formation of a revolutionary united front as its central task.

The Imperialist Powers and the Chinese Warlords At that time the political situation in China was characterized by constant wars between rival cliques of warlords, the imperialist powers backing one group against another according to which was more likely to benefit their particular interest.

The United States, Japan and Great Britain were the three principal imperialist powers taking part in the scramble for China after World War I. U.S. imperialism, having made fabulous profits out of the traffic in munitions and by loans to the belligerents, became the greatest exporter of capital. Searching for new sources of profit, it was inevitable that it should contend for the hegemony in the Pacific region. Japanese imperialism, taking advantage of the great war, had wrested more than any other power from China. Its special appropriations in China recognized at the Versailles Peace Conference, Japan was able to hasten its advance towards the exclusive control of China. U.S. imperialism and Japanese imperialism became the main rivals among the various imperialist powers for the domination and plunder of China. British imperialism had been the predominant power in China before World War I, but after 1918 its influence was practically at a standstill comparing with the advances then being made by the United States and Japan. Japanese imperialism's efforts to monopolize China were decidedly detrimental to British interests, and Britain sought the co-operation of the United States against Japan.

The Washington Conference, organized by the United States and supported by Great Britain, opened in November 1921. At this conference the United States and Great Britain jointly exerted pressure on Japan in the scramble for China. The Nine-Power Pact which resulted was signed in February 1922 by the United States, Belgium, Great Britain, China, France, Italy, Japan, the Netherlands and Portugal. This pact, which nominally respected the integrity of "China's sovereignty", was actually an agreement on its despoliation. It was based on aggressive principles, which the United States designated as "equality of opportunity for all the powers" and "the open-door policy". It abrogated the monopolistic rights which Japan had grabbed during the war, and substituted for it an arrangement whereby the United States, Great Britain and Japan jointly controlled China, U.S. imperialism taking the lead.

After the Washington Conference, and as a result of the concessions made by Japan under joint U.S.-British pressure, the conflicts between the three imperialist powers appeared to be less sharp. In point of fact, they continued, the difference being that they assumed new forms, principally by means of indirect intervention. Each power cultivated one or other of the Chinese warlords and used him as an agent to carry on wars for the expansion of its sphere of influence.

The Chinese feudal warlords became, in fact, the agents of imperialism in China. After the death of Yuan Shikai, the leader of the Beiyang warlords, in 1916, the Beiyang warlord group split into two cliques, known as the "Anhui clique" and the "Zhili (Hebei) clique". The Zhili clique was headed by Feng Guozhang and after his death in 1918, by Cao Kun and Wu Peifu. British and U.S. imperialists supplied the Zhili clique. The Anhui clique, headed by Duan Qirui, served as the lackey of Japanese imperialism. The Fengtian clique in the northeast, with the warlord Zhang Zuolin as its leader, also acted in collusion with Japan. These and other warlords represented the interests of various cliques of compradors and landed gentry at home. The struggles among the imperialist powers for the plunder of China were directly reflected in the interminable civil wars which raged among the rival warlords. Following the death of Yuan Shikai, the Anhui clique held the reins of power vested in the central government, which was situated in Beijing. In July 1920, fighting broke out between the warlords of the Zhili and the Anhui cliques at Yangcun and Zuozhou in Hebei Province. The Zhili clique came out on top, seized control of the Beijing government, and retained that position until October 1924. In April and May 1922, battles took place between the Fengtian and Zhili cliques in the Changxindian-Machang region of Hebei Province. The Zhili clique was again victorious. While the fighting was going on between the warlords in the north, a group of southern warlords conspired with their northern counterparts, with the result that civil wars also frequently occurred in the southern part of the country.

The Decision of the Communist Party of China to Form a Revolutionary United Front The intensified aggression of the imperialist powers, coupled with the internecine warfare between the warlords, made the life of the peasants almost intolerable. Oppressive levies and taxes were imposed on the peasants; these combined with the atrocities committed by warlords' soldiers, conscription, forced labour, natural and man-made calamities, increases in land rent and exorbitant rates of interest, caused widespread discontent and provoked struggles by the peasants. In south China peasant associations came into being, such as the General Peasant Association led by Peng Pai in Haifeng, Guangdong Province and the Yuebei Peasant-Worker Association led by Xie Huaide and Liu Dongxuan in Hengshan, Hunan Province. In the north the spontaneous struggles of the peasants for self-defence, like those of the Red Spear Society, grew in intensity.

As the exploitation of the workers was intensified, the political consciousness and unity of the working class developed.

When the imperialist powers renewed their economic aggression against China after 1922, industries operated by the national bourgeoisie, which had developed rapidly during World War I, gradually came to a standstill or faced a serious crisis. This was most conspicuous in China's textile and flour industries. From 1915 to 1921, China sold more wheat flour than it bought. The situation was reversed in 1922, and between five million and six million piculs were imported into the country annually in 1923 and 1924. As their plans for the development of industry were frustrated, the middle and petty-bourgeois classes became more conscious of the need for the abrogation of the unequal treaties which favoured the imperialist countries. They also opposed the civil wars waged by the warlords.

The cry for united action against imperialism and feudalism grew among all the revolutionary classes.

The Chinese Communist Party realized that if the revolution was to go forward, the organization of a broad-based revolutionary united front was necessary. In June 1923, the Party held its Third National Congress in Guangzhou. Thirty delegates, representing 432 members of the Party, attended. Among them were Li Dazhao, Mao Zedong, Chen Tanqiu, Qu Qiubai, Zhang Tailei, Cai Hesen and Xiang Jingyu. The discussion focussed on the question of the establishment of a national democratic and revolutionary united front, and the congress worked out a practical policy for its formation. It aimed to assist Dr. Sun Yat-sen, leader of the bourgeois revolutionary democrats, in the reorganization of the Kuomintang, and to allow members of the Chinese Communist Party and the Socialist Youth League to join the Kuomintang, so that it could become a revolutionary united front organization of the four classes — workers, peasants, petty bourgeoisie and national bourgeoisie. On this basis the revolutionary forces of the country could be united and organized for struggle. The congress also decided that the Communist Party should retain its own political and organizational independence. The Kuomintang had been formed in 1912, chiefly on the basis of the *Tong Meng Hui* (Chinese Revolutionary League) led by Sun Yat-sen.

Two extremist viewpoints emerged during the course of discussion at the Third Congress of the Communist Party. One was represented by Chen Duxiu, then the leader of the Communist Party, who held that the bourgeois-democratic revolution should be led by the bourgeoisie and that all the work of the Communist Party should be handed over to the Kuomintang. This was the Right capitulationist deviation. Another view was represented by Zhang Guotao,[1] who argued that the Communist Party must not co-operate with the Kuomintang

[1] Zhang Guotao was a renegade from the Chinese revolution. Inside the Party he made many mistakes which caused enormous losses. In the spring of 1938 he fled from the Shaanxi-Gansu-Ningxia Border Region to join the Kuomintang secret service.

and that only the working class could carry out the revolution. Zhang Guotao, therefore, opposed the idea that members of the Communist Party, workers or peasants should join the Kuomintang. This was the "Left" deviation or closed-door policy. These two views were opposed by Mao Zedong and others and finally rejected by the congress.

Mao Zedong was elected to the Central Committee of the Party at this congress, and became Director of the Organization Department under the Central Committee.

Sun Yat-sen Accepts the Aid of the Communist Party and Reorganizes the Kuomintang Thanks to the efforts of the Chinese Communist Party, the Kuomintang held its First National Congress in Guangzhou in January 1924 on the basis of co-operation with the Communist Party. The congress adopted the famous manifesto which accepted the anti-imperialist and anti-feudal basic principles as laid down by the Communist Party. It approved the "Three Cardinal Policies" of alliance with the Soviet Union, co-operation with the Communists and assistance to the peasants and workers. Sun Yat-sen's Three People's Principles were thus developed and became the New Three People's Principles, whose revolutionary essence was the Three Cardinal Policies. Members of the Communist Party who attended this congress included Mao Zedong, Li Dazhao, Lin Boqu and Qu Qiubai, all of whom were elected members or alternate members of the Kuomintang's Central Executive Committee. They played an important role at the congress. The formation of the revolutionary united front accelerated the upsurge of the revolutionary movement, and the First National Congress of the Kuomintang marked the beginning of this upsurge.

After the congress the Chinese Communist Party assisted Dr. Sun Yat-sen in establishing a military training school and in organizing a revolutionary army. This school, situated in Whampoa near Guangzhou, became known as the Whampoa Military Academy. The Communist Party sent Zhou Enlai, Ye Jianying, Nie Rongzhen, Yun Daiying, Xiao Chunü and Xiong Xiong to conduct political education at the academy, and many of the students were members of the Communist Party or Communist Youth League selected by the Party from all over the country, forming the revolutionary backbone there. In October 1924 the revolutionary army, with the assistance of the workers and peasants, suppressed the counter-revolutionary rebellion of the Guangzhou Merchant Volunteers, an armed force of the landlord and comprador classes of Guangdong Province, and strengthened the revolutionary regime in the province.

At this time, the Soviet Union consolidated friendly relations with the Chinese people by concluding a treaty on terms of equality with the Beijing government which still ruled a large part of China. Following repeated overtures by the Soviet Union, and under pressure of public opinion at home, the Beijing warlord government concluded on May 31, 1924 an agreement with the Soviet Union on general principles for the settlement of all issues between the Republic of China and the U.S.S.R. and established diplomatic relations with the latter.

The formation of the revolutionary united front gave a great impetus to the revolutionary mass movement in many parts of the land. The labour movement, which had been at a low ebb since the February 7th Massacre of 1923, revived and began to show signs of a new upsurge. The peasant movement in the Guangdong revolutionary base made rapid strides, while secret peasant associations developed in Hunan, Henan, Sichuan, Hubei, Jiangxi and other provinces.

The growth of the revolutionary united front brought about a split in the ranks of the Beiyang warlords. In October 1924, at the height of the war between the armies of the Zhili and Fengtian cliques, Feng Yuxiang of the Zhili clique led his troops back to Beijing and started a coup d'état. He broke away from the Zhili clique and declared himself in support of the revolution. The Zhili clique collapsed, and the central government in Beijing fell into the hands of the warlords of the Anhui and Fengtian cliques controlled by Japanese imperialism. The workers' and peasants' revolutionary movement in Chahar, Henan and part of Hebei, which came under the control of the National Army commanded by Feng Yuxiang, however, grew in strength. At this time the Chinese Communist Party launched a nationwide popular movement for the convening of a national assembly and the annulment of the unequal treaties imposed by the imperialist powers.

To greet the rising revolutionary upsurge, the Chinese Communist Party held its Fourth National Congress in Shanghai in January 1925; twenty delegates, including Li Dazhao, Zhou Enlai and Cai Hesen, were present, representing 980 members. The discussions of the congress focussed on the organizational work of the Party and its work among the masses. The congress decided to build and expand the Party organization throughout the country. It passed resolutions concerning the working class and the peasant movements, and decided on policies to be taken to lead the movement for the convocation of the national assembly. The congress made organizational preparations for the new upsurge of mass struggles.

In March of the same year, Dr. Sun Yat-sen died in Beijing. The whole nation was greatly distressed by the death of this great revolutionary democrat.

The May 30th Movement and Its Outcome There was a rapid development of the mass revolutionary movement after the Fourth National Congress of the Communist Party of China. A wave of strikes broke out among workers employed in Japanese-owned cotton mills in Shanghai and Qingdao. The Second All-China Labour Congress was convened in Guangzhou on May 1, 1925. It was decided to strengthen the leadership of the labour movement throughout the country, and in pursuance of this policy an All-China Federation of Trade Unions was set up with Lin Weimin and Liu Shaoqi as chairman and vice-chairman. On May 1, 1925 an All-Guangdong Peasants' Representative Conference was held in Guangzhou.

On February 9, 1925, more than forty thousand workers of Japanese-owned cotton mills in Shanghai went on strike in protest against the dismissal of Chinese workers. The workers were successful and the trade union organization made headway. The Japanese imperialists were determined to suppress the rising militancy of the Chinese workers and on May 14 the Japanese owners of a cotton mill unreasonably dismissed a number of its employees. A strike ensued. During the negotiation with the workers on May 15, the Japanese killed Gu Zhenghong, a Chinese labour delegate and a member of the Chinese Communist Party, and murdered and wounded ten of his fellow workers. This incident was the spark that led to the May 30th Incident. On that day two thousand workers and students publicly protested against the murders, against the proposed adoption by the Municipal Council of the "International Settlement" of the amendment to the by-law on printed matters, increase in wharfage dues and registration of the stock exchanges with the Municipal Council. These steps delivered a blow economically against the Chinese national bourgeoisie and evoked the indignation of the people in general. Several hundred students were arrested by the "International Settlement" police. Thereupon about ten thousand students and workers gathered in front of Laoza police station on Nanjing Road, where the arrested students were being held, and demanded their release. British police opened fire on the demonstrators, killing ten, seriously wounding fifteen, and arresting fifty-three others. This became known as the May 30th Massacre. Britain, Japan, the United States, Italy and France followed this up by bringing warships and a large number of marines to Shanghai. By June 4 the number of Chinese people killed and wounded by their armed forces amounted to a hundred and more.

The Nanjing Road massacre aroused tremendous feeling among the people of Shanghai and, responding to this, the Chinese Communist Party organized an "Action Committee" to lead this anti-imperialist struggle of the people. On May 31 the Shanghai Federation of Trade Unions was formed. It represented about 200,000 workers. From June 1 onwards, a wave of strikes began, involving more than 200,000 workers in Shanghai. Encouraged by the workers' actions, the majority of merchants closed their shops and fifty thousand students declared classroom strikes. The demonstrations continued and organization improved. On June 7, the Shanghai

Federation of Trade Unions, students from various colleges and schools and associations of medium and small businessmen organized a Joint Council of Workers, Businessmen and Students. This became the leading force in the movement against imperialism. The council submitted seventeen demands as a basis of negotiation with the imperialist powers, including an urgent request for the withdrawal of all imperialist armed forces from China. The presentation of the seventeen demands started a resolute struggle against imperialism.

Indignation against the May 30th Massacre spread all over the country. Workers downed tools, merchants closed shops and students stopped attending classes. Similar actions in protest against the massacre and in support of the people of Shanghai took place in Beijing, Hankou, Nanjing, Changsha, Tianjin, Jiujiang, Jinan, Fuzhou, Qingdao, Zhengzhou, Kaifeng, Chongqing, Hangzhou and Zhangjiakou. Peasants also backed the protest with demonstrations in the villages. Funds were raised to help the Shanghai strikers. There were clashes with the troops and police in many localities, and bloodshed ensued. A gigantic anti-imperialist revolutionary movement spread through the country.

The Consolidation of the Guangdong Revolutionary Base

The anti-imperialist movement reached its highest pitch in Guangzhou and Hongkong. In the latter city more than 100,000 workers, under the leadership of the Chinese Communist Party, declared a general strike on June 19 in support of the struggle of the Shanghai workers. Many of the Hongkong strikers went to Guangzhou, where all the workers in the British concession responded by walking out together. This became known as the Guangzhou-Hongkong Strike.

On June 23 the strikers and their supporters held a big march through Guangzhou. When the marchers arrived at Shakee (Shaji) in the Guangzhou suburbs, they were machine-gunned by British, French and Portuguese gunboats, soldiers and police. There were over two hundred casualties in this incident which subsequently became known as the Shaji Massacre.

This outrage further aggravated the anti-imperialist feeling of the people. On June 29 the number of strikers in Hongkong rose to 250,000. More than half of them left for Guangzhou with the result that the once prosperous city of Hongkong became a deserted port overnight. The strikers formed their own leading organization, the Guangzhou-Hongkong Strike Committee, and set up an armed picket corps of two thousand men. With the support of the Guangdong revolutionary government, pickets were posted at the various ports of Guangdong Province to enforce a blockade, and tribunals were set up to try traitors who had become the lackeys of imperialism. Led by the Chinese Communist Party and the well-known labour leaders Deng Zhongxia and Su Zhaozheng, and backed by the Guangdong revolutionary government and the peasants of that province, the strike lasted sixteen months. This was one of the longest strikes in the history of the world's working-class movement.

Thanks to the support of the more than 100,000 organized strikers, the Guangdong revolutionary base and its revolutionary government located in Guangzhou were further strengthened and consolidated. The National Government was inaugurated in Guangzhou on July 1, 1925. The various armies which had taken part in the revolution were reorganized and merged as the National Revolutionary Army.

Within one year, in 1925, the Guangdong revolutionary government and army wiped out all the counter-revolutionary forces in the province. In February and October they launched two Eastern Expeditions against the counter-revolutionary forces under Chen Jiongming entrenched in Chaozhou, Shantou and Huizhou. In June they routed the Yunnan and Guangxi troops stationed in the neighbourhood of Guangzhou, who were planning a revolt. During these campaigns the organized workers of Guangdong Province as well as the peasants under the leadership of the peasant associations rendered great assistance to the revolutionary forces. Members of the Chinese Communist Party and the Communist Youth League serving with the revolutionary army played a gallant and invincible vanguard role in these wars, greatly assisting in their speedy victory. Zhou Enlai was the General Director of the Political Department of the Eastern Expedition Army. After Chaozhou and Shantou were conquered, he became the Government Commissioner in this region, where he aroused the workers and peasants in a movement against the corrupt officials, local tyrants and evil gentry. By the spring of 1926 the whole of Guangdong Province was placed under the control of the revolutionary army.

It was about this time (December 1925) that J. V. Stalin foresaw that the Chinese revolution would develop with inestimable force. He wrote:

> The forces of the revolutionary movement in China are unbelievably vast. They have not yet made themselves felt as they should. They will make themselves felt in the future. The rulers in the East and West who

do not see these forces and do not reckon with them to the degree that they deserve will suffer for this.[1]

This prediction of Stalin's was based on a scientific analysis of the political and economic conditions and the balance of forces in China and the world. It was confirmed by the subsequent advancement of the revolutionary forces in China.

After the May 30th Movement, the peasant movement in Guangdong Province made rapid progress under the leadership of the Communist Party and the famous peasant leader Peng Pai. In May 1926 the Second All-Guangdong Peasants' Representative Conference was held in Guangzhou. It was reported that more than 620,000 people had joined the peasant associations. From May 1926, Mao Zedong was in charge of the well-known Guangzhou Institute of the Peasant Movement. The Communist Party selected a number of peasant movement cadres from twenty-one provinces and Inner Mongolia and sent them to the institute for training. Apart from Mao Zedong himself, Zhou Enlai, Xiao Chunü, Yun Daiying, Peng Pai, Li Lisan, Ruan Xiaoxian and others were invited to give lectures. Upon graduation the trainees went back to work in their own provinces, where many of them later became key cadres in the peasant movement.

The Right Wing of the National Bourgeoisie Plans to Usurp the Leadership of the Revolution In the period following the May 30th Movement the struggle for the leadership of the revolution became sharper between the members of the bourgeoisie and the proletariat within

---

[1] Stalin, *Works*, Vol. 7, Foreign Languages Publishing House, Moscow, 1954, p. 300.

the revolutionary camp. The right wing of the national bourgeoisie, fearing the growth of the workers' and peasants' movement and the rise in the Communist Party's political prestige, denounced communism and class struggle. A section of the right wing of the Kuomintang, which represented the influence of the landlords and compradors, then openly split off and formed the counter-revolutionary "Western Hills Conference Clique" (so named because in November 1925 they held a conference opposing the revolution in front of Sun Yat-sen's tomb[1] in the Western Hills outside Beijing). With the support of the Communist Party and the left wing of the Kuomintang, the Second National Congress of the Kuomintang, held in January 1926, took disciplinary action against this clique. The plans of the right wing of the national bourgeoisie as represented by Chiang Kai-shek to usurp the leadership of the revolution were however treated too lightly. At that period the Chinese Communist Party had not yet achieved a proper understanding of the need for proletarian leadership of the revolution. In March 1926, Mao Zedong clarified the question when he published his *Analysis of the Classes in Chinese Society*. In this, he pointed out that the industrial proletariat was the leading force in the Chinese revolution and that the peasantry was its largest and staunchest ally. He also pointed out that the national bourgeoisie, a vacillating class, would disintegrate during the upsurge of the revolution and that its right wing might become an enemy of the revolution. He called on the revolutionaries to be constantly on their guard to prevent the latter development. The article aimed primarily at the serious

---

[1] It was subsequently removed to Nanjing in 1929.

tendencies which then prevailed inside the Party. Right and "Left" opportunists in the leading organs of the Party ignored the peasants, did not know where to seek reinforcements, and felt helpless in face of the right wing of the Kuomintang.

Mao Zedong's correct views were not accepted by Chen Duxiu, a Right opportunist and the leader of the Party at the time. As a result, the leadership of the Party failed to adopt precautionary measures to combat the intrigues of the political representatives of the right wing of the national bourgeoisie who were lurking within the revolutionary camp and conspiring to attack both the Chinese Communist Party and the revolution in order to usurp leadership in the revolution. On March 18, 1926, Chiang Kai-shek conspired with his followers to order the cruiser *Chungshan,* commanded by a Communist, to proceed from Guangzhou to Whampoa. After the ship had left Guangzhou under his own order, Chiang Kai-shek spread the rumour that it had left without authorization and that its departure was designed to start an insurrection. On March 20 Chiang Kai-shek ordered his troops to arrest all the Communist Party members in the Whampoa Military Academy and in the First Army of the National Revolutionary Army. The premises of the Guangzhou-Hongkong Strike Committee and the residences of the Kuomintang's Soviet advisers were surrounded, and all Communist Party members were compelled to leave the ranks of the First Army of the National Revolutionary Army. The Right opportunists occupying leading positions in the Chinese Communist Party, headed by Chen Duxiu, adopted a compromising attitude towards this incident, and Chiang Kai-shek thereupon usurped the leadership of the National Revolutionary Army.

At the Plenary Session of the Central Executive Committee of the Kuomintang Chiang Kai-shek submitted on May 15 a "Resolution on Readjusting Party Affairs". This banned Communist Party members from positions of leadership in the various departments of the Central Headquarters of the Kuomintang. The adoption of this resolution further weakened the Communist Party's leadership in the Kuomintang, and Right opportunists within the Communist Party, headed by Chen Duxiu, made one concession after another, virtually encouraging the machinations of the right-wingers of the Kuomintang. Leadership in the revolution was gradually usurped by the right wing of the national bourgeoisie, endangering the great revolutionary movement against imperialism and feudalism.

The Victorious Progress of the Northern Expedition

Despite these drawbacks, the revolutionary movement continued to march forward. In July 1926 the National Revolutionary Army launched its Northern Expedition from Guangdong Province. It attacked the Beiyang warlords in three columns. This expedition was a revolutionary war jointly prosecuted by workers, peasants, the urban petty bourgeoisie and a section of the national bourgeoisie against imperialism and feudal forces. The Chinese Communist Party was the main driving force in this revolutionary war. The right-wingers, with Chiang Kai-shek and his like at their head, planned to step into the boots of the Beiyang warlords and attempted to turn the fight into a mercenary war for power in order to realize step by step their scheme for the betrayal of the revolution.

The Northern Expeditionary Army, with the full support of the masses of workers and peasants, advanced with lightning rapidity. Its main force, with the Independent Regiment commanded by Ye Ting, a member of the Communist Party, in the vanguard, drove through Hunan and entered Hubei. There in the south of the province it fought two bloody campaigns at Dingsiqiao and Heshengqiao. It occupied Hankou and Hanyang on September 7, 1926, and Wuchang on October 10, 1926. On January 1, 1927, the National Government moved from Guangzhou to Wuhan, the collective name for the three cities of Wuchang, Hankou and Hanyang on the Changjiang River.

On its eastern front, the Northern Expeditionary Army gained control of the whole province of Fujian in December, and then entered Quzhou in Zhejiang Province. The Expeditionary Army in Jiangxi, after repeated battles, captured Nanchang on November 8. In the north the National Army commanded by Feng Yuxiang moved southward from Suiyuan with the assistance of the Chinese Communist Party and gained control of the whole of the province of Shaanxi in December.

The rapid successes of the Northern Expedition were due to the fact that the war corresponded to the needs of the revolutionary situation and to the demand of the masses of the people. It also owed a measure of its success to the sympathy and support of the peoples of the Soviet Union and the whole world. The Expedition had the active support of the workers and peasants. When the Expedition started, the workers on strike in Guangzhou and Hongkong enrolled in large numbers and organized transport corps and teams of stretcher-bearers. The peasants and railway workers rendered great assistance when the expeditionary forces entered Hunan. Members of the Communist Party and Communist Youth League played a key and vanguard role in the units of the army. Under their political influence the warriors of the expedition fought heroically and strictly adhered to discipline.

Workers' and peasants' movements developed rapidly in the areas captured by the Northern Expeditionary Army. Trade union membership in the Wuhan area grew quickly and, by the beginning of 1927, it had reached 300,000, among whom armed picket corps were organized. Early in January 1927 the workers of Hankou and Jiujiang, acting in conjuction with the local people, drove out the British imperialists. With the support of the Wuhan National Government they occupied and took back the British concessions in the two ports. On March 21, 800,000 workers of Shanghai, led by Zhou Enlai, Luo Yinong and Zhao Shiyan (following two unsuccessful attempts in October 1926 and February 1927), launched a third armed uprising and succeeded in overcoming the armed forces of the feudal warlords. After two days and a night of furious fighting they occupied the city of Shanghai.

The influence of the Northern Expedition spread through the whole of the Changjiang valley and began to extend to the valley of the Huanghe River. At the same time, the peasant movement was growing in the southern provinces, particularly in Hunan, where several million peasants had joined the peasant associations and organized self-defence corps. The peasant associations led the local movements to overthrow the landlords and other feudal elements, and in some places actually confiscated their land. The slogan "All power to the peasant associations" was realized in numerous townships and villages.

The Views of Stalin and Mao Zedong on the Chinese Revolution In November 1926, when the revolution spread rapidly to the Changjiang River valley, the question of leadership in the revolution and its future development arose sharply. It was at that time that Stalin made his famous speech, *The Prospects of the Revolution in China,* at the Chinese Commission of the Seventh Executive Committee of the Communist International. He drew attention to the weaknesses of the Chinese national bourgeoisie and the serious danger of imperialist intervention against the Chinese revolution through the medium of Chinese counter-revolutionary forces. He urged the Chinese Communists to increase their vigilance. Stalin also pointed out that armed struggle was the principal and special feature of the Chinese revolution. He declared that it was extremely important for the Chinese Communists to have genuine revolutionary troops and to study the art of war. Moreover it was necessary to hasten and deepen the revolution in the countryside, so as to satisfy the demands of the peasants and strengthen the united front against imperialism. Stalin also pointed out that the proletariat must rise and control the leadership in the revolution and that the basic task of the Chinese Communist Party was to struggle for the non-capitalist future of the Chinese revolution.

The upsurge of the nation-wide peasant movement, with Hunan Province as its centre, had brought the struggle between revolution and counter-revolution to a very high pitch by the early part of 1927. Proletarian leadership in the revolution depended on whether the proletariat could support and lead the peasant movement.

A leadership of this kind was the only key to the success of the revolution. It was at this juncture that the Central Committee of the Chinese Communist Party sent Mao Zedong to Hunan to study the peasant movement. In March 1927 he published his work *Report on an Investigation of the Peasant Movement in Hunan,* which emphasized the important role of the peasantry in the Chinese revolution. He pointed out that revolutionaries must place themselves firmly at the head of the peasant movement, supporting and leading the peasants' struggles. He refuted and denounced the clamour of the reactionaries who slandered the peasant movement as being "terrible". He pointed out that the local tyrants, evil gentry and lawless landlords had formed the basis of autocratic government for thousands of years and were the cornerstone of imperialism, warlordism and the corrupt officialdom. The overthrow of this feudal power by the peasants who had risen in struggle was the real objective of the national revolution. His view was that the landlord class was deeply rooted, and that only by giving free rein to the peasantry and waging a thoroughgoing revolutionary struggle against feudalism, would it be possible to overthrow the landlord class. He further pointed out that after the landlords' power had been overthrown, peasant political power and a peasant army must be established to safeguard and develop the victories of the revolution. Mao Zedong's views were in sharp opposition to those of the capitulationists inside the Communist Party, headed by Chen Duxiu, who claimed that the working-class and peasant movements had gone "too far".

If the valuable opinions of Stalin and Mao Zedong had been accepted and put into force by the leaders of the Chinese Communist Party at that time, the revolution might have escaped defeat and continued to develop towards victory.

The Kuomintang Reactionaries Betray the Revolution

The national bourgeoisie were terrified by the tremendous advance made by the peasant and working-class movements. The imperialists, under the pretext that the rights of their residents and consulates in Nanjing had been violated, on March 24, 1927 bombarded the city, which had been liberated by the Northern Expeditionary Army. They also sent reinforcements to Shanghai to intimidate the national bourgeoisie. The Chiang Kai-shek clique, which represented the right wing of the national bourgeoisie, was then working hand in glove with the imperialists and the feudal and comprador forces in Shanghai. Chiang Kai-shek, in the interests of imperialism and the Chinese feudal and comprador classes, adopted bloody measures to suppress the revolutionary movement. On April 12, 1927, he launched a counter-revolutionary coup d'état in Shanghai, during the course of which many workers and Communist Party members were massacred. This was followed by further counter-revolutionary attacks in Guangzhou, Nanjing, Hangzhou, Ningbo and Fuzhou, in all of which large numbers of revolutionary workers, peasants and Communist Party members were arrested and killed. But because of the erroneous line of the Chen Duxiu elements in the leadership of the Chinese Communist Party, the Party lacked vigilance and failed to take precautions against betrayal by the Kuomintang reactionaries. Thus the revolutionary forces were unable to organize effective resistance against this sudden counter-revolutionary attack and met with a serious setback.

As a result of the counter-revolutionary coup d'état

of April 12, the First Revolutionary Civil War suffered a partial defeat. The national bourgeoisie then went over to the side of imperialism and the big landlord and comprador classes, and withdrew from the revolution. The imperialists and the big landlord and comprador classes hastened to use the Chiang Kai-shek clique as their new tool and established a counter-revolutionary government in Nanjing. With the desertion of the national bourgeoisie, the revolutionary camp became one of three classes — workers, peasants and the petty bourgeoisie — instead of four, and the revolutionary struggle entered a very critical stage.

On April 27, 1927 the Chinese Communist Party convened its Fifth National Congress at Wuhan. Eighty delegates attended, representing 57,967 members. Although the congress criticized the Right opportunist mistakes of Chen Duxiu, it re-elected him to the post of General Secretary of the Party, with the result that after the congress, Chen Duxiu continued to pursue his erroneous line of class capitulation. The congress failed to solve questions which cried for settlement: the question of land for the peasants, the questions of tactics towards the Kuomintang at Wuhan, of strengthening the revolutionary political power, arming the workers and peasants, and drawing up an economic policy.

After the congress the working-class and peasant revolutionary movement in Hunan and Hubei provinces, which were under the control of the Wuhan revolutionary government, continued to develop. The landlord class and the bourgeoisie, acting in support of the imperialists and Chiang Kai-shek's counter-revolutionary clique, staged a number of counter-revolutionary insurrections. On May 17, Xia Douyin, a reactionary officer, staged a revolt in Hubei. It was put down by Ye Ting's troops. On May 21, Xu Kexiang, another reactionary officer, staged a coup d'état in Changsha, Hunan, where many workers, peasants and cadres were massacred. The Wang Jingwei clique in Wuhan issued numerous directives for the repression of the popular revolutionary movement. The capitulationists headed by Chen Duxiu did not organize resistance to such adverse activities, but actually issued an order to disarm the workers and peasants. By compromise and concessions they attempted to win the support of Wang Jingwei. They abandoned the Communist Party leadership in the revolution, but subsequent events proved quite contrary to their expectations. For on July 15 the Wang Jingwei clique staged a counter-revolutionary coup d'état, and immediately proceeded to ban all popular organizations and carry out large-scale arrests and massacres of Communists, workers and peasants. The First Revolutionary Civil War which had been carried out by the Chinese people with such dynamic energy eventually failed.

The failure was due to the fact that the counter-revolutionary forces — the combined forces of imperialism and the reactionary clique of the Kuomintang — were far stronger than the revolutionary forces of that time. The Right opportunists in the leadership of the Communist Party, headed by Chen Duxiu, rejected the correct proposals of comrades represented by Mao Zedong within the Party. Nevertheless, the whole of the events of that year were of great historical significance and proved to be a valuable lesson for the revolutionary people. They enabled the Chinese people to realize that it was possible to defeat imperialism and the feudal forces. Moreover they witnessed the emergence of the Chinese

Communist Party as a revolutionary force fighting and sacrificing in the interests of the people, as the hope of the Chinese nation. The revolution also provided the Chinese working class and the Chinese Communist Party with rich practical experience and lessons, fostered and steeled a large number of Party cadres, who continued to lead the revolution forward. The First Revolutionary Civil War can be described as a "dress rehearsal" for the democratic revolution. It showed the Chinese working class and the Chinese people the way to victory.

II. THE SECOND REVOLUTIONARY CIVIL WAR (August 1927-June 1937)

The Crimes Committed by the Kuomintang Reactionaries

After the defeat of the First Revolutionary Civil War there was a realignment of class forces in the country. The national bourgeoisie went over to the comprador class and turned against the revolution, and a section of the petty bourgeoisie also broke away from it. The only classes which continued to fight for the revolution were the working class, the toiling peasants and the poor urban petty bourgeoisie. The imperialists, the feudal forces and the comprador class, using the Kuomintang reactionary clique as their new tool, established a counter-revolutionary military dictatorship — the rule of the Kuomintang new warlords — in place of the Beiyang warlords.

As the rule of Kuomintang new warlords headed by Chiang Kai-shek was established with the support of imperialism, this reactionary, traitorous clique capitulated to imperialism. Its main backing was the U.S. and

British imperialists, while at the same time bowing to the order of the Japanese imperialists.

The conflicts between the imperialists in their scramble for the Chinese market were reflected in the wars which henceforth continued for years between the various cliques of new Kuomintang warlords.

In the three years from October 1927 to 1930, there were seven large-scale wars between rival Kuomintang warlords and other opposing groups. In October 1927 there was fighting between Chiang Kai-shek and Li Zongren in Nanjing on one side and Wang Jingwei and Tang Shengzhi in Wuhan on another. In November, hostilities broke out between the Guangdong and Guangxi warlords for the control of Guangdong Province. In February 1928 there was a great battle for the control of north China between a coalition of four groups, headed respectively by Chiang Kai-shek, Li Zongren, Yan Xishan and Feng Yuxiang on the one hand, and Zhang Zuolin on the other. The former groups had the support of Great Britain and the United States, and Zhang Zuolin was supported by the Japanese. In March 1929 there was a war between Chiang Kai-shek and Li Zongren for the control of central China. In October of the same year Chiang Kai-shek declared war on Feng Yuxiang and two months later Chiang was attacked by Tang Shengzhi and Shi Yusan. In April 1930, Chiang launched a large-scale war in Henan against Yan Xishan and Feng Yuxiang. There were also frequent skirmishes between lesser warlords in Yunnan, Guizhou, Sichuan and Shandong. It is estimated that half a million men were killed in these internal wars, which spread over more than half of China and caused widespread misery among the civilian people.

All these wars ended in favour of Chiang Kai-shek. This was due to the fact that his faction, posing as the central government of China and the centre of the Kuomintang, obtained a large amount of aid from the United States and Great Britain, and internally the support of the Jiangsu, Zhejiang and Shanghai financial magnates. The imperialist powers supported the reactionary central regime of Chiang Kai-shek because they regarded it as an instrument for the repression of the revolution and the exploitation of the Chinese people. On the other hand they also followed a divide-and-rule policy by inciting and encouraging the local warlords in Guangdong, Guangxi, Sichuan, northwest and northeast China to maintain semi-independence, openly defying and even making war against the Nanjing government.

As internally it enjoyed the support of landlords, compradors and especially the financial magnates of Jiangsu and Zhejiang, the Kuomintang reactionary ruling bloc, headed by Chiang Kai-shek, was a united rule of landlords, compradors, warlords, bureaucrats, gangsters and Kuomintang party crooks. In essence, this regime was no different from that of the Beiyang warlords except that the new warlords of the Kuomintang, replacing the old warlords of the Beiyang type, seized the once-revolutionary Three People's Principles and the Kuomintang flag, and were now using them as a cover for their vicious fascist rule, which was more ruthless than that of the Beiyang warlords. Consequently the exploitation and repression of the people under this rule was more brutal than ever before.

As early as October 1928 Mao Zedong described the nature of this regime:

> The present regime of the new warlords of the Kuomintang remains a regime of the comprador class in the cities and the landlord class in the countryside; it is a regime which has capitulated to imperialism in its foreign relations and which at home has replaced the old warlords with new ones, subjecting the working class and the peasantry to an even more ruthless economic exploitation and political oppression.... Throughout the country the workers, the peasants, the other sections of the common people, and even the bourgeoisie, have remained under counter-revolutionary rule and obtained not the slightest particle of political or economic emancipation.[1]

This reactionary regime, the most barbarous in the world, carried out a savage and inhuman slaughter of the flower of the Chinese nation — the Communists and revolutionary youth. During the four or five years following the defeat of the 1927 revolution at least one million revolutionaries were murdered. Among them were outstanding leaders of the Communist Party, like Guo Liang, Cai Hesen, Chen Yannian, Zhao Shiyan, Xiao Chunü, Yun Daiying, Xiang Jingyu, Xiong Xiong, Peng Pai, Luo Dengxian, Luo Yinong, Wang Hebo, Chen Qiaonian, Xia Minghan, Sun Bingwen and He Mengxiong.

However, no matter what blood-thirsty measures the Chiang Kai-shek gangsters took, the Chinese people and the Chinese Communists could not be intimidated or wiped out. As Mao Zedong said:

---

[1] *Selected Works of Mao Zedong*, Foreign Languages Press, Beijing, 1975, Vol. 1, p. 63.

But the Chinese Communist Party and the Chinese people were neither cowed nor conquered nor exterminated. They picked themselves up, wiped off the blood, buried their fallen comrades and went into battle again. Holding high the great standard of revolution, they rose in armed resistance. . . .[1]

The August 1st Uprising and the Establishment of the Revolutionary Base in the Jinggang Mountains In order to retrieve the situation and continue the revolutionary struggle, Zhou Enlai, Zhu De, He Long, Ye Ting and Liu Bocheng, acting on the decision of the Central Committee of the Chinese Communist Party, organized an uprising at Nanchang in Jiangxi Province on August 1, 1927. This uprising of more than 30,000 men led to the establishment of a people's army under the leadership of the Communist Party, and unfurled a powerful revolutionary banner against imperialism and the reactionary rule of the Kuomintang. The troops which took part in the uprising, instead of joining forces with the peasant movement in Jiangxi, then proceeded southward towards Guangdong Province. They crossed Fujian and occupied Chaozhou and Shantou in Guangdong. Early in October they were defeated in a battle by the numerically superior Kuomintang forces. One section of the defeated troops moved into the Haifeng-Lufeng area and joined forces with the local peasant armed units. Another group, about a thousand strong, led by Zhu De, reached southern Hunan by a long and circuitous march. There they led a series of peasant uprisings and their ranks swelled to more than nine thousand. Later Zhu De and Chen Yi

---

[1] *Selected Works of Mao Zedong*, Foreign Languages Press, Beijing, 1975, Vol. III, p. 211.

led their men to the Jinggang Mountains, where they united with the forces under the command of Mao Zedong. These forces formed the nucleus of China's earliest Workers' and Peasants' Red Army.

On August 7, the Communist Party called an emergency meeting of its Central Committee at Hankou where it was decided to reject Chen Duxiu's Right capitulationist line and to set up a new leading committee. The meeting resolved that the Party must lead the people to continue the struggle against imperialism and feudalism, help the peasants in Hunan, Hubei, Guangdong and Jiangxi provinces to distribute the land of the landlords, and organize armed uprisings to overthrow the Kuomintang reactionary regime.

After the August 7th Meeting the Central Committee of the Chinese Communist Party sent Mao Zedong to eastern Hunan and western Jiangxi to organize an uprising at the time of the autumn harvest and to prepare for an attack on Changsha, capital of Hunan Province. By September Mao Zedong had brought together the peasant armies of Pingjiang and Liuyang, which had already participated in the uprising, the miners of Anyuan, and the guard regiment of the former National Government in Wuchang. This combined force became the First Division of the First Army of the Workers' and Peasants' Revolutionary Army. Before marching on Changsha this force attacked Liling, Liuyang and Pingjiang, but suffered setbacks. Assembling the defeated soldiers at Wenjiashi in Liuyang, Mao Zedong decided to abandon the plan to attack Changsha. Instead he and his men moved towards the middle section of the Luoxiao Mountain range to start guerrilla warfare. In October, after several difficult engagements, Mao Zedong led this force to the

Jinggang Mountains area situated on the border between Hunan and Jiangxi. There he established the first revolutionary base.

On December 11, Zhang Tailei, Ye Ting, Ye Jianying, Nie Rongzhen and other members of the Guangdong Provincial Committee of the Communist Party led an armed uprising of the workers and soldiers in Guangzhou. Between fifty thousand and sixty thousand men took part in it and a people's revolutionary regime was established in that city. This uprising was, however, crushed by the strong concentrated armed forces of the imperialists and the Kuomintang reactionaries.

Following the Nanchang and the Autumn Harvest uprisings, the Guangzhou Uprising was another action by the people which dealt a severe blow to the reactionary clique of the Kuomintang. Though it failed in the end, it marked a significant beginning in establishing the Red Army as did the two other uprisings.

In April 1928 the troops commanded by Zhu De joined with the forces led by Mao Zedong. The new army, totalling over ten thousand men, was named the Fourth Army of the Chinese Workers' and Peasants' Red Army. This force, composed of armed workers and peasants under proletarian leadership, was of an entirely new type. Its inauguration was an important event in China's revolutionary history. The Fourth Red Army carried out guerrilla warfare in the neighbourhood of the Jinggang Mountains, mobilized the peasants to carry out the distribution of land, set up a democratic regime of workers and peasants and effectively smashed three encirclement attempts by the forces of the Hunan and Jiangxi warlords.

The fact that Mao Zedong led the revolutionary armed force into the Jinggang Mountains proved to be of great historical significance. It combined the organized retreat from the cities, a result of the failure of the revolution, with new attacks on rural positions. In his celebrated article *Why Is It That Red Political Power Can Exist in China?* published in October 1928, Mao Zedong pointed out that in a semi-colonial country like China, which was under indirect imperialist rule, the incessant splits and wars between the various cliques of warlords created gaps, in which Red political power was able to rise and exist in the countryside despite encirclement by the White regime. He further pointed out that under correct leadership by the Party, and by integrating the wars fought by the Red Army with the agrarian revolution and the establishment of rural bases, the rural revolutionary bases could be gradually developed and expanded after a long period of revolutionary warfare, to encircle the cities and finally to achieve the nation-wide victory of the revolution. Mao Zedong's creative Marxist theory pointed out a new and correct road for the development of the Chinese revolution.

The Development of Revolutionary Bases The Sixth National Congress of the Communist Party was held in Moscow in July 1928, with 84 delegates representing over forty thousand members. The Congress summed up the experiences and lessons of the First Revolutionary Civil War period and reaffirmed that the Chinese society, after the defeat of the revolution, was still a semi-colonial and semi-feudal society, and that the Chinese revolution was still a bourgeois democratic revolution against imperialism and feudalism. The Congress pointed out that the political situation was then in a trough between two revolutionary upsurges. Outlining the general tasks of the Party, it said that the time was not opportune to launch offensives, nor organize uprisings, but that the task was to win over the masses to meet the oncoming revolutionary upsurge. The Congress approved a ten-point programme for the Chinese democratic revolution.

In spring 1929, Mao Zedong and Zhu De led the Fourth Army of the Chinese Workers' and Peasants' Red Army into southern Jiangxi. There they mobilized the people for guerrilla warfare and set up the Southern Jiangxi Revolutionary Base Area. From March to December of the same year, this army marched into Fujian three times to join forces with the Party organizations and uprising forces in western Fujian led by Guo Diren, Deng Zihui and Zhang Dingcheng. Together they established the Western Fujian Base Area. In July 1928, Peng Dehuai, Teng Daiyuan and Huang Gonglue led the Pingjiang Uprising, organized the Fifth Red Army and set up the Hunan-Hubei-Jiangxi Base Area. In winter 1927, Fang Zhimin, Shao Shiping and Huang Dao organized the Yiyang-Hengfeng Uprising. In summer 1930, they set up the Tenth Red Army and built the Fujian-Zhejiang-Jiangxi Base Area which later developed into the Central Revolutionary Base Area. Red Army forces totalling over 30,000 men were organized as the First Front Red Army with Zhu De as Commander-in-Chief and Mao Zedong as General Political Commissar. During the period from November 1927 to November 1928, guerrilla forces formed during the Huangan-Macheng Uprising led by Wu Guanghao, Pan Zhongru, Dai Kemin and Wu Huanxian and during the Shangcheng-Liuhe Uprising led by Zhou Weijiong, Qi Dewei and Xu Qishu developed into three Red Army devisions active in eastern Hubei, western Anhui and southern Henan respectively. Under the leadership of Zeng Zhongsheng and Xu Jishen, these areas were linked together as the Hubei-Henan-Anhui Base Area and the troops were organized as the First Red Army in spring 1930. Later this army and the Fifteenth Red Army in central Hubei formed the Fourth Front Red Army with Xu Xiangqian as Commander-in-Chief. In spring 1928, He Long, Zhou Yiqun, Lu Dongsheng and others returned to the border region between Hunan and western Hubei to join forces with the guerrilla under the command of He Jinzhai, Duan Dechang and Duan Yulin who had been waging a persistent struggle there. They built up the Fourth Red Army (later redesignated the Second Red Army) and the Sixth Red Army which were active along the Hunan-Hubei border and in the Hongze Lake area. Two years later, in 1930, these two armies joined each other in Gongan, merged as the Second Red Army Group, and set up the Hunan-Western Hubei Base Area. He Long was the Commander-in-Chief and Zhou Yiqun the Political Commissar of this army group. From December 1929 to February 1930, Deng Xiaoping, Zhang Yunyi, Li Mingrui and Yu Zuoyu led the armies which were under the influence of the Party and the peasant forces under the command of Wei Baqun in uprisings in Bose on the Youjiang River and Longzhou on the Zuojiang River in Guangxi. They organized the uprising forces as the Seventh and Eighth Red Armies and set up the Workers' and Peasants' Democratic Government there. In spring 1928, Liu Zhidan and Xie Zichang organized the Weinan-Huaxian Uprising and launched guerrilla warfare in Guanzhong and northern Shaanxi. Between 1929 and 1930 the Chinese Communist Party established a total of fifteen revolutionary bases of varied sizes in Hunan, Jiangxi, Fujian, Hubei, Anhui, Guangxi, Guangdong, Henan and other provinces. The centre of the revolutionary bases was in Jiangxi.

Under the leadership of the Chinese Communist Party the peasants enthusiastically carried out an agrarian revolution in districts where workers' and peasants' democratic political power was established and in places reached by the Red Army. The agrarian revolution proceeded along the lines laid down by the Party organization and Mao Zedong: Rely on farm labourers and poor peasants, unite with the middle peasants, restrict the rich peasants and eliminate the landlord class. Mao Zedong advocated the confiscation without compensation of the land and property of the landlords and their distribution to the peasants who had little or no land. The rich peasants were provided with a way out economically while the ordinary landlords were also allowed to make a living. Thus, in areas where the agrarian revolution was carried out, the feudal and semi-feudal system of exploitation was thoroughly overthrown and the peasants freed from such exploitation were active and tenacious in their defence of the revolutionary base areas and supported the Red Army. The Red areas were able to continue in existence for long periods and the Red Army was able to win continuous victories, mainly because of the active co-operation of the peasant forces.

The Chinese Workers' and Peasants' Red Army grew in strength with the correct leadership of the Chinese Communist Party and the support of the masses of peasants. By 1930 there were thirteen armies of the Red Army, totalling sixty thousand men, in different parts of the country. The principles for the building up of the Red Army stated that it was an army of workers and peasants under the absolute leadership of the Chinese

Communist Party; that it was a force guided by the class outlook of the proletariat, serving the people in their struggle and in the formation of revolutionary base areas. This army was a democratic one opposed to trends towards warlordism and the ways of roving rebels. The strategic and tactical principles of the Red Army stated that it must make the best use of the enemy's weak points and its own strong points. It must rely on the people's strength to the full. It must use guerrilla warfare and mobile warfare of a guerrilla character as its main form of fighting. Its strategy was one of protracted war, aiming to defeat the many with the few; its tactics were to wage battles of quick decision, to defeat the few with the many, so as to overcome the enemy and develop its own strength. Because the Chinese Workers' and Peasants' Red Army was built and waged wars according to the military line worked out by the Military Commission of the Party Central Committee and Mao Zedong, it was able to grow from a small and weak force into a large and strong one and eventually become a power which was at once indestructible, invulnerable and all-conquering.

The rapidity with which the Red Army developed was a serious challenge to the reactionary and traitorous rule of Chiang Kai-shek's Kuomintang. In December 1930 the reactionary troops of Chiang Kai-shek launched a large-scale campaign of "encirclement and suppression" against the Central Base Area in Jiangxi. Under the direction of the Party organization in the Central Base Area and Mao Zedong, the Workers' and Peasants' Red Army smashed three successive campaigns between the months of January and September in the year 1931. As a result, its strength further increased and the revolutionary base areas were extended.

In November 1931 the First National Congress of Workers and Peasants was held in Ruijin, Jiangxi Province. The Congress adopted a draft constitution, a labour law, an agrarian law and made many important decisions concerning the Red Army, the economic policy, the policy in regard to minority nationalities, and the establishment of a workers' and peasants' procuratorate. Mao Zedong was elected Chairman of the Executive Council of the Central Workers' and Peasants' Democratic Government of China and Zhu De was made Commander-in-Chief of the Red Army. Thus a united Central Workers' and Peasants' Democratic Government for the Red areas came into being.

The Occupation of Northeast China by Japan and the People's Struggle Against Japanese Aggression Towards the end of 1929, the capitalist world was plunged into the throes of an economic crisis. The monopoly bourgeoisie, seeking a way out, resorted to fascist dictatorships and intensified its repression of the working class and unleashed new wars for the redistribution of colonial holdings and spheres of influence. Japanese imperialism, in pursuance of its "continental policy" (which aimed at occupation first of northeast China and Mongolia, then the whole of China and the rest of Asia), began its aggressive campaign for the occupation of China's Northeast. On September 18, 1931, Japanese forces launched a surprise attack on Shenyang. Chiang Kai-shek's Kuomintang adopted a policy of "non-resistance", with the result that the three northeastern provinces of Liaoning, Jilin and Heilongjiang with two million square kilometres of territory and a population of more than thirty million were lost to the Japanese in three months' time. The following year, the Japanese imperialists set up a puppet "Manchukuo" government to control this area.

Japan's seizure of northeast China caused a new upsurge in the people's movement for national independence and democracy. The Communist Party and the Workers' and Peasants' Red Army were the first to raise the slogan of resistance against Japan. The people took up this call and demanded action against Japanese aggression. In the Northeast they organized anti-Japanese volunteer corps to carry out resistance. In Shanghai, Guangzhou, Hongkong and other centres, workers staged anti-Japanese strikes, and there was a nation-wide voluntary boycotting of Japanese goods. Anti-Japanese rallies and demonstrations were organized by the people in numerous cities and townships.

Japan's aggression against China brought about changes in the relationship between various classes within the country. The national bourgeoisie which had hitherto depended on Chiang Kai-shek's Kuomintang, began to express dissatisfaction with its policy of "non-resistance" to Japan. In December 1931, thirty thousand students from Shanghai, Beiping, Tianjin and Nanjing gathered in the latter city to protest against the Kuomintang's sell-out of northeast China and to demand resistance to Japan. They were suppressed by Chiang Kai-shek's Kuomintang. This sanguinary action aroused great anger among people in all sections of society.

The British, French and American imperialist powers played the role of accomplices in the Japanese aggression against China. They organized a League of Nations Commission to carry out a so-called "investigation" on the spot. Following this "investigation" the Commission recommended that northeast China should be placed under "international control". This recommendation was virtually an encouragement to Japan to attack the Soviet Union from the vantage-point they had secured in northeast China. The Soviet Union under the leadership of Stalin was the only country which upheld justice and firmly denounced Japanese aggression.

The Japanese imperialists, attempting to subjugate China at one stroke, launched a surprise attack on Shanghai on January 28, 1932. Inspired by the rising anti-Japanese sentiment of the people in the whole country, the troops of the 19th Route Army under the command of Cai Tingkai and stationed in Shanghai resisted the attack in defiance of Chiang Kai-shek. The Communist Party mobilized the workers and students of Shanghai, and organized volunteer corps to participate in the fighting at the front and to carry on work behind the lines in support of the army. The people of Shanghai and other parts of the country raised funds to support the defenders. All this was of great assistance to the 19th Route Army. After more than a month of heroic struggle the Shanghai defenders suffered defeat as a result of the traitorous actions taken by Chiang Kai-shek's Kuomintang.

After the Kuomintang's betrayal of the Shanghai battle, the nation-wide movement which had arisen following the Japanese occupation of northeast China was temporarily suppressed. Nevertheless it asserted itself sporadically in places. In May 1933, three military commanders, Feng Yuxiang, Fang Zhenwu and Ji Hongchang (the latter a member of the Communist Party) organized the Chahar-Suiyuan Anti-Japanese Allied Army in Zhangjiakou. They recaptured Duolun, Baochang, Guyuan and other places. In November of the same year, some patriotic elements among the Kuomintang, including Li Jishen, Chen Mingshu and Cai Tingkai, established an Anti-Japanese People's Government in Fujian where they co-operated with the Red Army to resist Japan and oppose Chiang Kai-shek. They were subsequently suppressed by Chiang Kai-shek assisted by the Japanese aggressors.

The Long March of the Red Army In June 1932 Chiang Kai-shek assembled a force of 500,000 men for its fourth campaign of "encirclement and suppression" against the revolutionary bases. By February the next year Chiang Kai-shek's offensive had again been smashed by the Central Red Army which fought heroically under the command of Zhou Enlai, Zhu De and Nie Rongzhen. The gravity of the national crisis deepened day by day and in order to unite all the armed power in the country in a common effort to repel the Japanese invaders, the Workers' and Peasants' Democratic Government and the Red Army issued a manifesto on January 17, 1933. It expressed willingness to co-operate with all troops who wanted to resist Japan and to cease attacks on the Red Army, and were prepared to arm the masses of the people and safeguard their democratic rights. There was a favourable response from a section of the patriotic military leaders in the Kuomintang including Feng Yuxiang, Li Jishen and Chen Mingshu as mentioned above. Chiang Kai-shek's Kuomintang, however, replied to this righteous call by continuing to yield to Japan and by preparations for an even larger-scale campaign of "encirclement and suppression" against the Red Army. With the support of the United States, Britain, Japan, Germany and Italy, Chiang Kai-shek unleashed his fifth big campaign of "encirclement and suppression" against the revolutionary bases in October 1933.

In the counter-campaign against Chiang Kai-shek's attack, the "Leftists" headed by Chen Shaoyu and Qin Bangxian in the central leading organ of the Communist Party at that time brushed aside the military line formulated by Mao Zedong. They carried out a line based on passive defence, and committed a number of other mistakes. This policy and other consequential mistakes made it impossible for the Red Army to smash the enemy's encirclement despite its gallant defence which went on for more than a year. In this situation, the Red Army had no alternative but to embark on a big strategic shift of position. On October 16, 1934, the main force of the Red Army left the Jiangxi revolutionary base, broke through the enemy cordons, and began its celebrated Long March. Some of the guerrilla units, commanded by Xiang Ying and Chen Yi, were left behind to continue guerrilla warfare against the enemy in that area. Though it subsequently had to carry out many difficult struggles, this force was able to retain its revolutionary strength and later became the nucleus of the New Fourth Army.

In January 1935 the Red Army after passing through Guangdong, Hunan and Guangxi arrived at Zunyi in Guizhou Province. There the Chinese Communist Party convened an enlarged conference of the Political Bureau of the Central Committee. Addressing the conference, Mao Zedong, who based his arguments on the realistic lessons learned from experiences during the war, convinced and won over many comrades. The conference put an end to the incorrect "Left" line of the Central Committee, endorsed the correct policy advocated by Mao Zedong, elected a military command group composed of

Mao Zedong, Zhou Enlai and Wang Jiaxiang, and established the leading position of Mao Zedong in the Central Committee.

At the Zunyi Conference, it was decided to continue to march northward to resist Japan. After passing through Yunnan and making a detour round the border between Sichuan and Xikang, the Central Red Army arrived at Maogong, in northwestern Sichuan, in June. There it linked up with the Fourth Front Red Army which had withdrawn from the Sichuan-Shaanxi Revolutionary Base. Together they pushed further northward, crossing the Great Snow Mountains and arriving at Maoergai in the vicinity of Songpan. There Mao Zedong led the Party and the Red Army in opposition to the criminal activities of Zhang Guotao, who aimed to split the Party and the Red Army.

The Central Red Army continued its northward advance. After surmounting incredible difficulties, crossing the marshlands, and fighting hard and bitter battles in the provinces of Gansu and Shaanxi, it arrived at the Northern Shaanxi Revolutionary Base in October 1935. There it united with the local Red Army units. Thus ended the 25,000-li Long March, a feat rare in the whole of human history. In October 1936 part of the Second and Fourth Front Red Armies led by He Long, Ren Bishi, Guan Xiangying and Xiao Ke also arrived in northern Shaanxi to join the Central Red Army.

The Long March of the main forces of the Red Army which covered eleven provinces and traversed over 25,000 li took exactly a year. The Red Army, during the course of the march, defeated 411 Kuomintang regiments with a total strength of several hundred thousand men. It defeated all their attempts to overtake, encircle, intercept and annihilate it. The men of the Red Army scaled the Five Ridges and the high mountains and steep peaks of Wumeng. They conquered the natural barriers of the Wujiang River, Jinsha (Golden Sand) River and Dadu River. They climbed the Great Snow Mountains, a land of everlasting snow. They marched across the vast uninhabited marshlands and forced the dangerous Lazikou Pass. Overcoming difficulties and hardships beyond human imagination, but receiving the support of the people all along their route, including valuable help from minority peoples such as the Miaos, Yis, and Tibetans, the Red Army victoriously completed its historic mission. The victorious conclusion of the Long March demonstrated that the Chinese people's forces, led by the Communist Party, were unconquerable. It steeled the main force of the Red Army, and the cadres of the Party. It inspired the people of the whole country, and brought the nationwide anti-Japanese democratic movement to a new upsurge.

The Anti-Japanese National United Front Begins to Take Shape The Four Big Families of Chiang Kai-shek, T. V. Soong and H. H. Kung (both related to Chiang by marriage) and of his faithful associates, Chen Guofu and Chen Lifu, took advantage of their political position to batten on the blood, sweat and toil of the people of the Kuomintang-ruled area. Economically, with the support of British and American imperialists, they constituted the bureaucrat monopoly-capitalist rule of the Four Big Families. Politically, they organized a colossal fascist secret police organization and instituted a fascist-style police terror for the suppression of all anti-Japanese and revolutionary activities. They continued their treacherous concession policy in dealings with the

Japanese aggressors. In May 1933, they signed the "Tangku Agreement" which gave *de facto* recognition to Japan's occupation of the four northeastern provinces of Liaoning, Jilin, Heilongjiang and Rehe. Two years later, in May 1935, they concluded the "Ho-Umezu Agreement", which was tantamount to recognition of the right of the Japanese invaders to dominate and control north China.

The sell-out of China's sovereignty by Chiang Kai-shek's Kuomintang caused the national crisis to become more serious than ever before. In November 1935 the Japanese aggressors instigated Chinese traitors to engineer the "East Hebei Incident", in which a puppet political regime was set up in the twenty-two counties of eastern Hebei. At the same time, the Japanese started a bogus "autonomy" movement for north China, which they used for the purpose of extending their aggressive influence to the whole of north China.

This crisis of national subjugation provoked the left wing of the Chinese national bourgeoisie into a more open expression of anti-Japanese sentiments. Divergent views on the question of resisting or surrendering to Japan were also evident within the Kuomintang camp. The Chinese Communist Party, taking into consideration the new changes in the class relations in the country in the face of Japanese imperialist aggression, and also acting in accordance with the policy of the Communist International concerning the formation of a united front against fascism and imperialism, on August 1, 1935 issued an "Appeal to Fellow-Countrymen Concerning Resistance to Japan and National Salvation". This appeal proposed a cessation of civil war and united action against Japan. In December 1935 the Central Committee of the Chinese

Communist Party adopted a "Resolution on the Present Political Situation and the Tasks of the Party". This endorsed the Party's Anti-Japanese National United Front policy. Mao Zedong published a report entitled *On Tactics Against Japanese Imperialism,* in which he systematically explained this new policy.

The demand for national salvation and survival advanced by the various classes and strata of the Chinese people found expression in the December 9th Students' Patriotic Movement. At the call of the Communist Party, and under its leadership, Beijing students staged a mighty demonstration on December 9, 1935. They demanded resistance to Japan and called for national salvation, and expressed determined opposition to the anti-Communist civil war. On December 16 a much larger demonstration took place. These two demonstrations awakened response throughout the country, and gave a fresh stimulus to the anti-Japanese democratic movement. Similar demonstrations were then held by students, workers and residents in Hangzhou, Tianjin, Shanghai and other cities. This led to the formation of National Salvation Associations in Shanghai and other centres. Periodicals, pamphlets and leaflets in support of resistance to Japan and for national salvation mushroomed into existence. The developing and deepening of the anti-Japanese national salvation movement prepared a popular basis for the subsequent War of Resistance Against Japan.

After the fall of northeast China, the fight of the Northeast Anti-Japanese Volunteers developed rapidly under the leadership of the Communist Party. In 1934, in accordance with the directives of the Central Committee of the Chinese Communist Party, the various groups of anti-Japanese armed forces in northeast China were unified and reorganized into seven units called the Northeast Allied Anti-Japanese Army. In 1935 they were expanded into eleven army corps and one independent division. In 1936 the various units were reorganized into three groups to fight a guerrilla warfare on three fronts. The Northeast Allied Anti-Japanese Army, battling against the ruthless oppression of the Japanese invaders and circumstances of extreme hardship, heroically carried on a long struggle against the invaders. The people of northeast China supported the struggle of the Allied Army in every possible way, taking on every kind of risk. They regarded the Allied Army as their hope, and its leaders, Yang Jingyu and Li Hongguang, were greatly respected by the people. The struggle of the Northeast Allied Army inspired and stimulated the anti-Japanese feeling of the people throughout the country.

The Communist Party's call for an anti-Japanese national united front, and the growth of the anti-Japanese national salvation movement, had a great impact on a section of the Kuomintang army. Early in 1936 the troops of the Kuomintang Northeast Army under Zhang Xueliang, and those of the 17th Route Army under Yang Hucheng, which had been ordered by Chiang Kai-shek to "suppress the Communists" in northwest China, virtually suspended operations against the Red Army after negotiations between Zhou Enlai and Zhang Xueliang at Yanan. They established friendly relations with the Red Army on the basis of resistance to Japan. On December 12, they refused to accept Chiang Kai-shek's orders to attack the Red Army. In a swift surprise action they arrested Chiang Kai-shek and detained him in Xian. They presented him with eight demands, including a demand for the cessation of civil war and co-operation with the Communists to resist Japan. The Communist Party, mindful of the serious national crisis, advocated peaceful settlement of the incident on condition that Chiang Kai-shek agreed to national unity and resistance to Japan. For this purpose, the Chinese Communist Party sent Zhou Enlai, Qin Bangxian and Ye Jianying to Xian as its representatives. Chiang Kai-shek was released after having been forced to accept these conditions. The Chinese Communist Party's policy in this incident met with the support of the people throughout the country.

The Xian Incident, as it came to be called, was a turning-point in the situation. The civil war which had lasted nearly ten years, virtually came to an end and a new period began. It was marked by internal peace and preparations for resistance to Japan. After the September 18th Incident, the national contradiction between Japan and China had gradually become the main one, and contradictions between the Chinese people and the other imperialist powers, as well as the contradictions between the various classes inside China gradually fell into a subordinate position. The Japanese invasion of north China, with the threat to subjugate the whole of China, was a challenge to the interests of Britain and the United States, and both these imperialist powers wanted China to adopt a stiffer attitude towards Japan. This influenced the pro-British and pro-American elements among the Chinese big bourgeoisie represented by Chiang Kai-shek. This fact, coupled with the strong pressure from the people, compelled these elements to accept a policy of alliance with the Chinese Communist Party for resistance against Japan, and the anti-Japanese national united front called for by the Communist Party began to take shape. This united front included the pro-British and pro-American elements within the big bourgeoisie. In the spring of 1937 the Communist Party put forward a new programme, which called for "consolidation of internal peace, democracy, and the realization of resistance to Japan".

At this time Mao Zedong was engaged in the preparation of several outstanding theoretical works. His *Problems of Strategy in China's Revolutionary War,* written in 1936, and his philosophical works, *On Practice* and *On Contradiction,* written in 1937, summed up and analysed the experiences of the Chinese revolution during the period of the Second Revolutionary Civil War and made important contributions to the Communist Party's Marxist-Leninist ideological and military lines.

During the ten years of the Second Revolutionary Civil War, the Chinese people under the leadership of the Chinese Communist Party continued to push forward the great revolutionary cause against imperialism and feudalism. The struggles and sacrifices of numerous Communist Party members, non-party revolutionaries and revolutionary people form an epic story which will be inspiring for all time. During this period the Chinese people accumulated a wealth of revolutionary experience, particularly in the waging of the people's revolutionary war. The work of integrating the theory of Marxism-Leninism with the practice of the Chinese revolution as exemplified by the theoretical writings of Mao Zedong also made great progress. The ten years of hard struggle steeled the Chinese Communist Party and its cadres, hardened and preserved the powerful Chinese Workers' and Peasants' Red Army and safeguarded the Shaanxi-Gansu-Ningxia Revolutionary Base Area. All these factors finally became the mainstay and the advance position of the revolution from which it was possible to organize and win the War of Resistance Against Japan.

III. THE WAR OF RESISTANCE AGAINST JAPAN (July 1937-September 1945)

Resistance Led by the Chinese Communist Party The depression which enveloped in the capitalist countries after 1933 was followed by a new economic crisis in the second half of 1937. The fascist countries, Germany, Japan and Italy, all frantically carried out a policy of aggressive war. Japanese imperialism sought to convert China into a colony for its exclusive exploitation. It launched a fierce attack at Lugouqiao Bridge, on the southwestern outskirts of Beijing on July 7, 1937. The local Chinese garrisons courageously resisted. The following day the Communist Party issued a manifesto to the whole nation calling for armed resistance. After considerable wavering and hesitation, the pro-British and pro-American bloc, composed of big landlords and big bourgeoisie within Chiang Kai-shek's Kuomintang, was finally compelled to offer resistance to Japan. They did so partly because of pressure from the people and partly because the Japanese offensive had seriously endangered the interests of the British and U.S. imperialists and also the financial interests of the Four Big Families. In August, the main force of the Red Army in the Shaanxi-Gansu-Ningxia Border Region changed its name to the Eighth Route Army, and left for the north China battlefield to fight against the Japanese aggressors. The Eighth Route Army, 45,000 strong, had Zhu De as commander, Peng Dehuai as deputy commander, Ye Jianying as chief of staff, Zuo Quan as deputy chief of staff and Ren Bishi as director of general political department. It had three divisions: the 115th Division, with Lin Biao as commander and Nie Rongzhen as political commissar and deputy commander; the 120th Division, with He Long as commander, Guan Xiangying as political commissar and Xiao Ke as deputy commander; the 129th Division, with Liu Bocheng as commander, Deng Xiaoping as political commissar and Xu Xiangqian as deputy commander. In September the Kuomintang and the Chinese Communist Party formally announced their renewed co-operation. This meant the formal establishment of the Anti-Japanese National United Front, initiated and led by the Communist Party. Shortly afterwards the Red Army guerrilla units in the south were reorganized as the New Fourth Army. This army then proceeded to fight the Japanese on the central China battle front. The New Fourth Army, 15,000 strong, had Ye Ting as commander, Xiang Ying as political commissar and deputy commander, Zhang Yunyi as chief of staff, Zhou Zikun as deputy chief of staff, Yuan Guoping as director of political department and Deng Zihui as deputy director of political department. It had four detachments: the 1st Detachment, with Chen Yi as commander; the 2nd Detachment, with Tan Zhenlin as commander; the 3rd Detachment, with Zhang Yunyi as commander; and the 4th Detachment, with Gao Jingting as commander.

After the outbreak of the war, there were two differing lines of policy because of the existence of two differing political forces in the camp of resistance. One force, that of the big landlords and big bourgeoisie, was headed by the Four Big Families. It acted in their interests and those of British and American imperialism, and took a line of passive resistance, prepared for compromise with Japan. The other force, that of the proletariat and the great mass of the people, was headed by the Communist Party. It took the line of waging a people's war and a struggle for complete victory. On July 23, Mao Zedong published an article entitled *Policies, Measures and Perspectives for Resisting the Japanese Invasion,* in which he pointed out that there were two policies, two measures and two perspectives dealing with the prosecution of the anti-Japanese war. One policy, he said, was that of a resolute resistance. Those who were sincere about this policy must adopt the policy of relying upon the masses of the people and the perspective for them was the achievement of China's liberation. On the contrary, if the policy was not to be one of resolute resistance but of compromises and concessions, and not to be one of reliance on the people, the only possible perspective was that the Chinese people were to become slaves and beasts of burden. Mao Zedong called on the people of the whole country to oppose the latter and to fight for the realization of the first policy and bring about the realization of victory in the people's War of Resistance. On August 25 the Chinese Communist Party made the first policy the basis of its "Ten-Point Programme for Resistance to Japan and the Salvation of the Nation". The Programme gave the people a clear-cut objective and mapped out the only possible way of struggle for victory.

Because of the anti-popular line of the Chiang Kai-shek bloc, the Kuomintang troops suffered one reverse after another during the first six months of the War of

Resistance. At the end of 1937 the Kuomintang troops in north China had fled from Beijing and Tianjin southward to the neighbourhood of the Huanghe River. At the same time the Kuomintang troops in central China retreated from Shanghai and Nanjing westward towards Wuhan. In December the Chiang Kai-shek clique began to waver, and through the intermediary of the German ambassador, entered into negotiations with Japan. The Communist Party's strong opposition to any compromise or surrender, coupled with the rising anti-Japanese feeling of the people, frustrated this move for compromise with the enemy.

There was a sharp contrast in the situation on the battle fronts. The Kuomintang forces simply melted away before the advance of the enemy, but the Communist-led Eighth Route Army and New Fourth Army, guided by the policy of the people's war, attacked the rear of the enemy both in north and central China and won a series of victories. In September, the Eighth Route Army wiped out more than three thousand men of the crack Itagaki Division in the Pingxingguan Pass in Shanxi Province. This victory was a great encouragement to the anti-Japanese movement throughout the country. The Eighth Route Army and the New Fourth Army continued to harass the enemy's rear wherever it went. They mobilized the people and developed guerrilla warfare, establishing anti-Japanese democratic bases behind the enemy lines in the provinces of Shanxi, Chahar, Hebei, Suiyuan, Shandong, Henan, Anhui and Jiangsu. Under the leadership of the Communist Party, popular administrative organizations consisting of coalitions of various anti-Japanese democratic classes were formed in these various democratic bases. The people were organized and armed on a broad scale. A policy of rent reductions and lower rates of interest was carried out, and the people's standard of living was improved. All this stimulated the people to take action in the War of Resistance, and in this way the struggle behind the enemy lines played a very important and active role in the war against the Japanese aggressors. In the first year of the war, 300,000 Japanese troops were pinned down and subjected to attacks from the rear.

In order to refute two erroneous views, which were very much in vogue in the Kuomintang camp at the time, namely, the "theory of national subjugation" and the "theory of quick victory", to expound the Communist Party's correct policy guiding the War of Resistance, and to direct the people to think along the line of fighting a protracted war and achieving the final victory in the war, Mao Zedong, in May 1938, drew up a treatise entitled *On Protracted War*. Analysing the basic characteristic of the contradictions which existed between the enemy and the Chinese people, he pointed out that the War of Resistance would be a protracted one but that the Chinese people would surely win the ultimate victory if they exerted their efforts. He forecast that the war would pass through three stages, namely, the stage of strategic defensive, the stage of strategic stalemate and the stage of strategic counter-offensive. Mao Zedong defined a whole set of military principles for guidance in the people's War of Resistance Against Japan and formulated the brilliant strategic plan of developing the people's war in order to make the War of Resistance culminate in a victory for the people. This outstanding theoretical work played an important role in the subsequent victory of the people's War of Resistance.

In October 1938, the Chinese Communist Party convened the enlarged Sixth Plenary Session of its Sixth Central Committee in Yanan. The session decided to make the ideas expounded by Mao Zedong in his book *On Protracted War* the guiding principle in its pursuance of a protracted war of resistance. At the same time, the session criticized the capitulationist ideas of Wang Ming (Chen Shaoyu) and others inside the Party towards the Kuomintang. It once again pointed out that the proletariat must maintain the principles of independence in the Anti-Japanese National United Front, assume the responsibility of leading the national war, and resolutely carry out the policy of both unity and struggle within the united front. The session decided that the Party should concentrate its work mainly in the war zones and the enemy's rear, and that the Party must exert its utmost effort to organize the armed struggles of the people against Japan.

The Japanese invaders occupied Guangzhou and Wuhan at the end of October 1938, and the Kuomintang forces retreated to the mountainous regions of the southwest, making Chongqing their centre. The growing fighting strength and size of the Communist-led Eighth Route Army and New Fourth Army, and the establishment of anti-Japanese bases in the rear of the enemy were a serious threat to the Japanese. The aggressors suspended their attacks on the Kuomintang troops in order to divert their main forces to north and central China to deal with the Eighth Route Army and the New Fourth Army. This marked a great change in the war situation, and henceforth the Japanese rear became the principal battleground, the two sides holding one another at bay for long periods by a series of bitter, intensive combats. The fighting between the Japanese and the Kuomintang came almost to a standstill, consisting mainly of intermittent skirmishes. The War of Resistance reached the stage of stalemate.

Help from the Soviet Union; Britain's and the United States' Attempt to Induce the Kuomintang to Come to Terms with Japan After the outbreak of the War of Resistance, the Soviet Union, led by Stalin, was the only foreign country that genuinely assisted China in its war against Japan. On August 21, 1937, the Soviet Union signed a mutual non-aggression treaty with China, a guarantee of powerful friendly support. By the end of 1941 Soviet assistance in the form of loans and munitions was estimated to be valued at about five times the total amount of loans from Britain, the United States and other countries. It was the Soviet Union which aided China in the darkest and most difficult days of the war.

The policy of Britain and the United States at that time was "to sit on the mountain and watch the tigers fight". They rendered just sufficient aid to China to enable the two "tigers", the Chinese people and Japanese imperialism, to fight it out. They looked on and made enormous profits out of the sale of war materials. The United States supplied Japan with most of the petrol, aeroplanes, copper and iron and steel used by that country in its aggressive war against China. Ninety-two per cent of the war materials used by Japan during the year 1938 was supplied by the United States. Britain and the United States hoped that when China and Japan were both exhausted, they would be able to force China to come to terms with Japan and then make Japan concede to some of their demands. In this way they would be able to reap the advantages without much trouble.

During the winter of 1938 and the spring of 1939, foreign press agencies repeatedly issued reports stating that the British and American governments were prepared to sponsor a so-called "Pacific International Conference" to "mediate" in the Sino-Japanese conflict. The British ambassador to China, Sir Archibald Clark Kerr, made frequent journeys between Hongkong, Chongqing and Shanghai carrying on "mediation" activities. The Japanese imperialists' policy towards the Kuomintang then changed from that pursued during the first stage of the war. Military offensive, which had been the main feature of their policy, was now of secondary importance. They used political pressure to bring about Chiang Kai-shek's capitulation. A series of statements designed to tempt Chiang Kai-shek into making a deal with them was issued by the Japanese government. These statements greatly strengthened the forces of compromise and capitulation within the Kuomintang-controlled areas.

The Chinese Communist Party Persists in the War of Resistance and Checks Three Anti-Communist Onslaughts by the Kuomintang At this time the greatest obstacle to the capitulationist activities of the Kuomintang was the Communist Party and the anti-Japanese forces led by it. The Kuomintang ruling clique adopted a passive attitude towards the War of Resistance and acted like spectators placidly watching its outcome. They were actually preparing for surrender and concentrating their main strength against the Communists and the people to that end. On July 7, 1939, the Chinese Communist Party issued a manifesto, calling on the people of the whole country to persist in the War of Resistance and to oppose capitulation; persist in unity and oppose splits; persist in progress and oppose retrogression.

During the winter of 1939 and the spring of 1940, the armed forces of the Kuomintang attacked the Shaanxi-Gansu-Ningxia Border Region and the anti-Japanese democratic bases in Shanxi. This was the first anti-Communist onslaught during the period of the War of Resistance. The military and civilian population of the anti-Japanese democratic bases replied by delivering resolute counter-blows against the invaders. They acted in accordance with the principles laid down by the Central Committee of the Communist Party, including the general principle of "developing the progressive forces, winning over the middle forces and isolating the die-hard forces"; the principle of resolute self-defence — "we will not attack unless we are attacked; if we are attacked, we will certainly counter-attack"; and the principle of waging struggles against the Kuomintang reactionaries: "On just grounds, to our advantage, and with restraint". This first anti-Communist onslaught was beaten back and the danger of capitulation was temporarily removed.

When the War of Resistance entered the stage of stalemate, the fighting in the enemy's rear was intensified. Following what they called a "prison-cage method", the Japanese invaders proceeded to blockade and chop up the anti-Japanese bases into small areas. They followed this up with a series of what they termed "mopping-up operations". The military and civilian population of the anti-Japanese democratic bases valiantly and repeatedly smashed the enemy's encirclement, enlarging the bases and developing its own strength. By 1940 the population of the anti-Japanese democratic base areas had increased to 100,000,000, the military forces led by the Communist Party had reached 500,000, and the membership of the Communist Party had grown to about

800,000. The period between the outbreak of the War of Resistance and 1940 was a period of great development for the anti-Japanese forces under the leadership of the Communist Party.

In January 1940, Mao Zedong issued his celebrated work dealing with the question of the Chinese revolution, *On New Democracy*. Its purpose was to arm the Chinese Communist Party and the anti-Japanese people with correct theory and well-guided policies, as well as to rebut the fascist anti-Communist thesis of the Kuomintang reactionaries who claimed that conditions in China permitted the existence of only "one party, that is, the Kuomintang, one doctrine and one leader". Mao Zedong, on the basis of Marxist-Leninist theory and the practical experience of the Chinese revolution, made a comprehensive explanation of the Communist Party's theory and policy on the Chinese revolution and the political, economic and cultural reconstruction of China. He pointed out that the victory of the War of Resistance would be a victory for the people and for a new democracy, and proved that the fascism of the Kuomintang reactionaries was doomed. This book provided the Communist Party and the people with a clear-cut ideological programme.

Chiang Kai-shek, seeking to co-operate with the Japanese invaders for the destruction first of the New Fourth Army and then of the Eighth Route Army, unleashed his second anti-Communist onslaught in October 1940. The following January, eighty thousand Kuomintang troops made a surprise attack on the headquarters of the New Fourth Army in southern Anhui. Ten thousand men fought back courageously but the greater part of them were killed, including Deputy Commander Xiang Ying, Director of Political Department Yuan

Guoping and Chief of Staff Zhou Zikun. Commander Ye Ting was arrested while at negotiations with the Kuomintang forces. This is what has come to be known as the "Southern Anhui Incident".

Immediately after this slaughter, the Japanese invaders and the troops of Wang Jingwei (who openly surrendered to Japan in December 1938 and became president of the bogus national government in Nanjing in 1940) acted in concert with Chiang Kai-shek in launching attacks on detachments of the New Fourth Army stationed in various localities in central China. Chiang Kai-shek moved large bodies of troops in preparation for another large-scale attack on the Communist-led forces. The Communist Party adopted a firm revolutionary policy. On January 20, 1941, the Military Commission of the Party Central Committee issued an order on rebuilding the New Fourth Army, appointing Chen Yi its acting commander, Zhang Yunyi its deputy commander and Liu Shaoqi its political commissar. The New Fourth Army was reorganized into seven divisions: the 1st Division, with Su Yu as commander; the 2nd Division, with Zhang Yunyi as commander; the 3rd Division, with Huang Kecheng as commander; the 4th Division, with Peng Xuefeng as commander; the 5th Division, with Li Xiannian as commander; the 6th Division, with Tan Zhenlin as commander; and the 7th Division, with Zhang Dingcheng as commander. The Chinese Communist Party exposed the treachery of the reactionaries to the people of the whole country, and called on them to prevent this betrayal. The New Fourth Army and the whole population of the various anti-Japanese democratic base areas were mobilized under emergency orders. Preparations were under way to repulse the combined attacks of the Kuomintang troops and the Japanese invaders. The masses of people, and democratic elements within the ranks of the Kuomintang — notably Soong Ching Ling and He Xiangning — opposed and protested against the criminal conduct of Chiang Kai-shek. The second anti-Communist onslaught was finally defeated, and Chiang Kai-shek was completely isolated from the people.

The anti-Japanese democratic base areas were in dire straits in 1941 and 1942, because of the continued ruthless attacks of the Japanese invaders, their puppet troops and Kuomintang forces. The fascist camp had temporarily gained an upper hand on the battlefield after Hitler's attack on the Soviet Union in June 1941 and in the early stages of the war in the Pacific which started in December of the same year. The Japanese invaders, attempting to transform north and central China into a rear base for a world-wide offensive, intensified their terrorist colonial rule in the occupied areas of China, and systematically stripped them of material resources. Fiercer, bigger and more frantic "mopping-up" campaigns were launched against the anti-Japanese base areas. They used the most barbarous measures in carrying out a policy of "burn all, kill all and loot all", endeavouring to completely destroy the anti-Japanese democratic base areas by creating a desolate "no man's land". At the same time, the Kuomintang forces intensified their encirclement, blockade and destruction of these areas. The Kuomintang even sent large numbers of their troops over to the enemy, to be used as puppet forces, directly co-operating with the Japanese in attacks on the anti-Japanese forces. Under the combined blockade and "mopping-up" operations of the enemy, the puppet troops and Chiang Kai-shek's forces, the anti-Japanese democratic base areas diminished in size, their military forces were reduced, and the people and the armed forces all suffered great privations. Despite conditions of extreme hardship, the anti-Japanese armed forces and the people continued their heroic struggles, and the Communist Party adopted a number of practical measures to overcome these difficulties, tide over the crisis and consolidate the base areas. In order to cope with the financial and economic difficulties, including those arising from the provisioning of the soldiers and civilians, the whole army and people in the Liberated Areas were mobilized in a large-scale operation for production. At the call of Mao Zedong, all military units, government institutions, schools and civilians organized themselves into groups to reclaim waste land, develop subsidiary agricultural enterprises and engage in handicraft production. In this way many armed units became completely or partially self-sufficient and government institutions and schools managed to provide themselves with most of the food and clothing they required. In the intensified struggle against the enemy, militia units and armed working corps were organized on a broad scale for the purpose of concentrating attacks on small groups of enemy forces. Various types of home-made weapons and means of warfare were improvised to fight the enemy. The enemy troops were harassed by land-mine operations in the mountains and by "tunnel warfare" on the plains. At the same time the burden on the peasants was lightened by the policy of rent and interest reduction, which enabled them to develop their own initiative in support of the War of Resistance. Efforts were made to rally as many people as possible to fight the enemy.

The policy of "fewer and better troops and simpler administration" was put into force to save the financial and material resources of the base areas and lighten the burden on the people. Efforts were made to unify the leadership of the anti-Japanese base areas, to establish a democratic government and to enlighten the people on current affairs. The army was called on to support the government and help the people in every possible way. The Party, government and people were in turn called upon to support the army and give preferential treatment to the families of those engaged in combat duties. The Communist Party convinced the people that the existing difficulties were but the "dark hour before the dawn", and called on them to "clench their teeth" and push on through the darkness to greet the dawn of victory.

During this difficult period, the Communist Party launched a rectification movement to improve the Party's style of work and thereby strengthen its fighting power. The Party cadres studied the basic principles of Marxist-Leninist dialectical materialism and the fundamental principles formulated by Lenin and Stalin in regard to the role of the Communist Party. They were encouraged to proceed from reality in doing everything and integrate theory with practice. They applied criticism and self-criticism in order to overcome any tendencies towards subjectivism, sectarianism and stereotyped Party writing. This rectification movement enabled the Party to achieve a new unity on the ideological basis of Marxism-Leninism, with the result that the Party underwent a profound change. Thus the Party proceeded to lead and organize the masses of people more effectively in the carrying out of their struggles.

The victory of the Soviet Red Army in the battle for

Stalingrad, early in February 1943, was a turning point in World War II. From then on, the world anti-fascist camp composed of the Soviet Union, the United States, Britain and other countries shifted from the defensive to the offensive. Under the brilliant leadership of the Chinese Communist Party and Mao Zedong and by the correct application of well-thought-out policies, the Chinese Liberated Areas surmounted an extremely difficult situation and commencing from 1942 succeeded in smashing through ruthless encircling attacks by the enemy. The Liberated Areas gradually began to recover and extend.

The Kuomintang launched its third anti-Communist onslaught during June and July of 1943. It withdrew its large army stationed on the bank of the Huanghe River and directed it towards the Shaanxi-Gansu-Ningxia Border Region. The Kuomintang troops shelled its defence positions along the river and prepared a nine-pronged attack on Yanan, the capital city of the border region and the seat of the Central Committee of the Chinese Communist Party. At the same time the Kuomintang clamoured for the "dissolution of the Chinese Communist Party". The Communist Party exposed in advance the Kuomintang's plans and denounced its policy. The entire military and civilian population of the border region had been successfully mobilized and engaged in active preparations to repel the prepared invasion. Public opinion throughout the whole country had also been alerted in opposition to the Kuomintang.

The Communist Party Fights for Anti-Japanese Democracy Under these combined pressures, the anti-Communist onslaught was again forestalled. By 1944, the forces of the Liberated Areas were waging limited counter-offensives and the areas had once more begun to expand. In north, central and south China there were fifteen anti-Japanese democratic base areas with a total population of over 80,000,000. They had 470,000 regular troops, in addition to a people's militia of 2,270,000. The membership of the Communist Party was well over 900,000, and the material conditions of the people in the Liberated Areas had markedly improved as a result of the further development of the movement for production. The armed forces and the people of the Liberated Areas became the main force in the subsequent victory of the War of Resistance.

The Kuomintang-controlled areas had become an abyss of degeneracy and corruption. The Kuomintang reactionary leaders, headed by the Four Big Families of Chiang Kai-shek, T. V. Soong, H. H. Kung and Chen Li-fu, had reached a position where they were able to dominate the whole economic system and impose heavy tolls on the people. They issued unlimited quantities of notes, cornered supplies and smuggled goods to the enemy-controlled areas, frantically plundered the Chinese people and amassed fantastic amounts of wealth for themselves. Feudalistic, comprador and military monopoly capital — known as bureaucrat capital — rapidly accumulated under the control of the Four Big Families. The degenerate and corrupt Kuomintang's civil and military functionaries, big and small, indulged in widespread embezzlement, blackmail and extortion by force. This, coupled with the grain shortage that occurred year after year, and the absence of material resources caused by the Japanese blockade, made the lot of the ordinary people almost unbearable. Kuomintang secret police rode roughshod over the people, who were allowed no political freedom whatsoever. Tens of thousands of progressive young men and women were thrown into Kuomintang fascist concentration camps and subsequently slaughtered. This tyrannical and corrupt rule brought about widespread dissatisfaction in the Kuomintang-controlled areas and mass uprisings took place in many places.

The Japanese invaders, having fallen into an unfavourable position in their war against the Allied Powers in the Pacific, unleashed a new campaign in the Kuomintang-controlled areas in March 1944. This campaign, known as the Henan-Hunan-Guangxi campaign, was aimed at opening a line of communications from north China to Burma and India. The demoralized Kuomintang troops collapsed in a panic-stricken retreat before this offensive, and by the end of the year had allowed the enemy to penetrate as far as Dushan in Guizhou Province. Chongqing was shaken. The debacle of the Kuomintang army and the dark fascist rule of the Kuomintang gave rise to a new high tide in the patriotic democratic movement of the people in the Kuomintang-controlled areas. The people of Chongqing, Kunming and other districts organized rallies and demonstrations, where they demanded the repeal of the fascist political and military orders, the abolition of Kuomintang dictatorship and the establishment of a democratic coalition government.

In September 1944 the Chinese Communist Party raised the call for the reorganization of the national government and the supreme command and the formation of a democratic coalition government. This call received the enthusiastic endorsement of all the democratic parties and groups and also of people from all social strata. The demand was however rejected by the Kuomintang. The

United States had by now taken advantage of the War of Resistance to further dominate the Kuomintang government and troops. The American representatives and Chiang Kai-shek attempted to complete the alleged "unification" and "democratization" of the Kuomintang government by inviting certain Communists to participate in the government. They hoped, by this means, to sidetrack the demand for the reorganization of the Kuomintang government into a democratic coalition government, and also to destroy the Eighth Route Army and the New Fourth Army and the Liberated Areas. This vicious proposal by the United States and Chiang Kai-shek was resolutely rejected by the Chinese Communist Party. The various democratic parties and groups and the broad masses of the people also saw through it, and recognized the reactionary role of the United States and Chiang Kai-shek.

The Seventh National Congress of the Chinese Communist Party The Chinese Communist Party convened its Seventh National Congress at Yanan on April 24, 1945. It was attended by 544 delegates and 208 alternative delegates, representing 1,210,000 members. The Congress unanimously adopted Mao Zedong's political report *On Coalition Government*, which analysed the international and domestic situation, summed up the experience of the Party in leading the new-democratic revolution in the previous two decades or more, especially the experience in the two-line struggle during the War of Resistance, and formulated for the entire Party and nation a comprehensive programme and a correct line for defeating the aggressors and building a new China. The Congress also listened to Zhu De's military report *The Battle Front of the Liberated Areas* and Liu Shaoqi's organizational report on revising the Party constitution. The Seventh Party Congress showed unprecedented unity. It adopted a new constitution and elected a new Central Committee headed by Mao Zedong.

At the Congress it was reported that the Chinese people, under the leadership of the Communist Party, had already created nineteen Liberated Areas with a total population of 95,500,000 people. The People's Liberation Army numbered 910,000 men, including the Eighth Route Army, the New Fourth Army and the South China Anti-Japanese Contingent, and there was a militia of 2,200,000 men who were engaged in production as well as fighting. The People's Liberation Army had turned to a partial counter-offensive since 1944. The majority of the leading cities and lines of communications were besieged or controlled by the People's Liberation Army. It was now obvious that victory in the War of Resistance and in the cause of democracy could be ensured by relying on the mighty People's Liberation Army and on the unity of the people of the whole nation. The Congress called upon the whole Party and the people throughout the country to struggle for final victory in the War of Resistance and for the establishment of a democratic coalition government.

The Victory of the War of Resistance On May 2, 1945, the Red Army of the Soviet Union entered Berlin and Hitler's Nazi gang surrendered unconditionally. This ended the anti-fascist war in Europe.

On August 8, 1945, the Soviet Union declared war on Japan. The following day the Soviet Red Army, moving with lightening rapidity, attacked and penetrated, by four routes, into the strategic base of the Japanese invaders in northeast China. On August 10, the People's Republic of Mongolia declared war on Japan. The Japanese invaders' most important strategic base collapsed, and more than one million picked Kwantung troops melted away before the onslaughts of the valorous Red Army.

On August 9, Mao Zedong issued a statement, calling on the people to launch a final all-out offensive against the Japanese. On August 10 General Zhu De, Commander-in-Chief of the Chinese People's Liberation Army, issued an order to the troops in the Liberated Areas, commanding them to disarm the Japanese troops in their respective areas within a specified period. The troops of the Chinese People's Liberation Army in the various Liberated Areas were then mobilized for a big offensive against cities and towns and lines of communications controlled by the Japanese.

On August 14, Japan announced its unconditional surrender, formally signing the documents on September 3. After eight years of hard struggle by the Chinese people, the War of Resistance ended in victory.

Many large Chinese cities and main lines of communications were heavily besieged and encircled by the People's Liberation Army at the time the surrender was announced, and the Japanese forces should have surrendered directly to the People's Liberation Army. The troops of the Kuomintang had withdrawn far into the interior, in southwest China. The Kuomintang authorities, however, under the direction of the United States, decided to rob the people of the fruits of their victory in the War of Resistance. They connived with the Japanese and puppet troops and ordered them to resist the People's Liberation Army. The U.S. forces assisted in the air and sea transport of Kuomintang troops to "take over" the cities and lines of communications, and to attack the People's Liberation Army. A new civil war was provoked.

After eight years of bitter struggle in which millions of people gave their lives, the Chinese people at last defeated the ferocious Japanese imperialism and won victory in the sacred War of Resistance. The Chinese Communist Party was the organizer and leader of this victorious people's war. It had led the people in waging a life-and-death national liberation war against an external foe — Japanese imperialism — and had carried out an unflinching revolutionary struggle against the anti-Communist and anti-popular line of the Kuomintang reactionaries inside the resistance camp. A great victory had been obtained in this dual struggle. The victory of the people led by the Communist Party in the War of Resistance paved the way for victory in the Third Revolutionary Civil War.

IV. THE THIRD REVOLUTIONARY CIVIL WAR (September 1945-September 1949)

The Communist Party Struggles for Peace and Democracy

After the War of Resistance ended, the Kuomintang, representative of the big landlords and big bourgeoisie, planned to seize the people's fruits of victory in the war and to establish a dictatorial rule throughout the country. They used the military strength they had built up in the interior during the war and the foreign arms they had received to unleash a large-scale civil war, their purpose being to wipe out the Chinese Communist Party and all the revolutionary forces of the people. After the Japanese surrender, the United States aimed to gain control of

China's extensive markets and to convert it into an American colony, collaborating with the Kuomintang for the carrying out of this plan. The Chinese people were now faced with the serious problem of civil strife.

Having experienced eight bitter years of war, the Chinese people wanted peace and a democratic way of life. The Communist Party, representing the interests of the people, led the struggle for internal peace and democracy. On August 25, 1945 the Communist Party issued a "Declaration on the Current Situation". It called on all the people to bring about national unification on the basis of peace and democracy and unity, and demanded the immediate realization of peace and the avoidance of civil war.

On August 28, Mao Zedong went to Chongqing, the site of the Kuomintang government, and entered into negotiations with it. After more than a month of persistent struggle, the Kuomintang government was finally compelled to recognize the principles of peace and democracy. On October 10, the two sides signed an agreement and announced that "civil war must be averted at all costs". The agreement provided for the calling of a political consultative conference to discuss fundamental plans for the peaceful reconstruction of the country.

After the publication of the agreement, the Communist Party, in accordance with its terms, withdrew its troops from eastern Zhejiang, southern Jiangsu and southern Anhui. But even while the negotiations were in progress, the Kuomintang was making secret dispositions of their troops, preparing for a five-pronged attack on the Liberated Areas. No sooner had the agreement been signed than it dispatched a large force against the Liberated Areas in the Shangdang region in Shanxi Province and the Handan region in Hebei Province. During the last twenty days of October the People's Liberation Army successfully combated this attack, and the Kuomintang lost 110,000 troops. This was a crushing blow against the Kuomintang's plot to unleash a new civil war.

Defeated in its first military offensive, the Kuomintang discovered that its preparations for a large-scale civil war were incomplete. Meanwhile, the Communist Party was waging a resolute struggle for peace and democracy. For these reasons the Kuomintang, under the pressure of domestic and international opinion, signed a truce agreement with the Communist Party on January 10, 1946. Both sides issued a cease-fire order. General George C. Marshall, the U.S. president's special representative, posed as a peace "mediator" in the "military mediation" between the two sides. He thereby enabled the Kuomintang to gain time for the deployment of its military forces. On the same day that the truce agreement was signed, a Political Consultative Conference opened at Chongqing. Delegates of the Communist Party and the China Democratic League and non-party democratic personages attended the conference. The Communist Party submitted many constructive proposals to the conference and succeeded in uniting the democratic forces of the country in a common struggle against the Kuomintang plot for a new civil war. Under pressure of public opinion the Kuomintang found itself politically isolated and devoid of initiative. It was therefore compelled to make certain concessions to the people. As a result, the conference adopted several resolutions which were, at the time, favourable to the cause of peace, democracy and unity.

The Chinese Communist Party and the Chinese People Smash the Attacks of the Kuomintang Troops The

Kuomintang, which had participated in the Political Consultative Conference against its will, regarded the holding of the conference and its resolutions as a political defeat for itself. It violated the truce agreement, while the conference was in session, by moving large bodies of troops to the civil war fronts in readiness for attack. After the conference closed, it called a plenary session of its Central Executive Committee and expressed its opposition to the resolutions it had just endorsed. Shortly afterwards it brazenly broke the truce agreement and tore up the decisions of the Political Consultative Conference. Throughout this period it never ceased its attacks on the Liberated Areas in northeast China. In April and May it once more launched a large-scale campaign there. George C. Marshall and other U.S. representatives, who were taking part in the work of "military mediation" in the guise of "mediators", were actually doing everything possible to help Chiang Kai-shek in the deployment of his troops for civil war. The United States transported large numbers of Chiang Kai-shek's troops by air and sea to points from which attacks could be launched on the Liberated Areas. It supplied Chiang Kai-shek with large quantities of munitions and war materials, and equipped and trained his men. Chiang Kai-shek unleashed a large-scale civil war mainly because of the encouragement and support given to him by the United States.

Meanwhile the Chinese Communist Party continued its efforts for peace, but the Kuomintang, relying on American aid, construed these efforts as a sign of weakness and rejected them. The Kuomintang instructed its special agents to suppress the patriotic democratic movement and redoubled the persecution of the democratic leaders.

All this exposed the treachery of Chiang Kai-shek and the United States in their lip-service to "peace". The Chinese people gradually woke up from their peace dream to the need of overthrowing the Kuomintang ruling clique to achieve peace, democracy and independence.

On June 26, 1946 Chiang Kai-shek assembled an army of 300,000 men and launched a campaign of encirclement against the Liberated Areas of the central plain on the Hubei-Henan border. Sixty thousand men of the Central Plain Liberation Army led by Li Xiannian, Zheng Weisan and Wang Zhen broke this encirclement and took up new positions.

This was followed in July by an all-out offensive by Chiang Kai-shek's troops against all the Liberated Areas. In this offensive Chiang Kai-shek employed 1,600,000 regular forces who were technically supported, aided, and advised by U.S. experts. From all directions the enemy penetrated into the Jiangsu-Anhui, Southern Shanxi, Southwestern Shandong, the Shandong Peninsula, Eastern Hebei, Eastern Suiyuan, Southern Chahar, Rehe and Southern Liaoning Liberated Areas. Thus the Chiang Kai-shek bloc, with the support of the United States, embarked on a civil war on a scale unprecedented in the history of China.

At the outset of this war the total strength of Chiang Kai-shek's army was 4,300,000, while the Chinese People's Liberation Army had only 1,280,000 men. The Kuomintang, relying on its numerical superiority and military aid supplied by the United States, adopted the strategy of an all-out offensive, frantically attacking and seizing cities and territory, hoping thereby to quickly destroy the people's Liberated Areas. This offensive reached its peak in the early part of 1947.

Faced with this situation, the Communist Party and Mao Zedong drew up carefully thought-out political and military plans to cope with it. They demonstrated that, on the political front, it was necessary to organize and lead a broad united front of the whole population against Chiang Kai-shek and his ally, the United States. Dealing with the military situation, they pointed out that, in the face of the offensive by the enemy who enjoyed temporary numerical superiority, the Chinese People's Liberation Army should adopt the strategy of mobile defence, making the annihilation of the enemy's effective strength, and not the defence of cities, towns or localities, the main objective.

The People's Liberation Army correctly carried out the military principles defined by the Party Central Committee and Mao Zedong. At the outbreak of the war the soldiers and civilians of the various Liberated Areas were mobilized. Mobile defence was organized to smash Chiang Kai-shek's attacks. Within a period of eight months, the People's Liberation Army voluntarily abandoned some important towns in the Liberated Areas, such as Zhangjiakou in Hebei Province, Chengde in Rehe Province and Huaiyin in Jiangsu Province, but in the course of its manoeuvres, it put 700,000 enemy troops out of action. The People's Liberation Army armed itself with the equipment it captured from the enemy, and swelled its ranks with prisoners of war converted to the people's cause. Thus the People's Liberation Army became larger and stronger as the fighting continued, while the Kuomintang troops grew fewer in number and weaker in fighting morale. For this reason, the Kuomintang found itself compelled, after March 1947, to stop its all-out offensive and start concentrated offensives on the eastern and western flanks of the Liberated Areas — the Shandong and northern Shaanxi battle fronts. It also decided to switch over to the defensive on other fronts. The Northwest Field Army led by Peng Dehuai, He Long and Xi Zhongxun and the East China Field Army led by Chen Yi and Su Yu smashed concentrated enemy offensives by flexible tactics. The People's Liberation Army began a partial counter-offensive in northeast and north China.

The Fight for the Thorough Destruction of the Feudal and Comprador Regime After a year of mobile defensive warfare the People's Liberation Army had put 1,120,000 of Chiang Kai-shek's troops out of action and expanded its own regular forces from 1,280,000 to 2,000,000 men. From July to September 1947 the People's Liberation Army went on the offensive on a nation-wide scale and shifted the major battle fronts onto the Kuomintang-controlled areas. This was a reversal in the strategic positions of the two opponents, the People's Liberation Army shifting from strategic defensive to strategic offensive, while the army of Chiang Kai-shek, which had suffered heavy losses in effective strength, was forced to switch from strategic offensive to strategic defensive. It was also a turning point in history. In his report *The Present Situation and Our Tasks*, made at a session of the Central Committee of the Communist Party in December of the same year, Mao Zedong pointed out: "It is the turning point from growth to extinction for Chiang Kai-shek's twenty-year counter-revolutionary rule. It is the turning point from growth to extinction for imperialist rule in China, now over a hundred years old."[1]

---

[1] *Selected Works of Mao Zedong*, Foreign Languages Press, Beijing, 1977, Vol. IV, p. 157.

This report also expounded the Party's military strategy, its policies for land reform, the rectification movement of the Party, its economic policy, questions concerning the people's democratic united front and other questions.

The fact that an agrarian reform had been carried out inside all the Liberated Areas was another fundamental reason why the People's Liberation Army was able to beat back the offensive of the Kuomintang forces. After Japan's surrender the peasantry had voiced an urgent demand for land. To meet this demand, the Communist Party had issued a directive on May 4, 1946, which changed the policy from one of reducing rent and interest to that of confiscation of the land of the landlord class to be distributed among the peasants. In September 1947 the Communist Party drew up the Outline Land Law of China. This provided for the abolition of the old landownership system of feudal and semi-feudal exploitation, and put the system of "land to the tillers" into effect. After this, a large-scale land reform movement was carried out in the old and semi-old Liberated Areas. In one year after the promulgation of the Land Law, about 100 million peasants in the Liberated Areas received land. This gave a great impetus to their participation in and support for the liberation war and greatly assisted in the consolidation of the rear of the people's forces.

The Upsurge of the Patriotic Democratic Movement in Kuomintang-Controlled Areas As Chiang Kai-shek's anti-popular civil war proceeded, the colonization of the Kuomintang-controlled areas deepened, the economic crisis grew more serious, and the people's patriotic democratic movement against Chiang Kai-shek and his United States backers developed in intensity.

After the Japanese surrender, the bureaucrat-capital of the Four Big Families, who constituted the Kuomintang ruling oligarchy, was boosted by the take-over of the wealth and property of the Chinese people which had been accumulated by the Japanese invaders through long years of ruthless plunder and exploitation. At the same time, the Four Big Families subordinated their own interests to those of American monopoly-capital and reduced the economy of the Kuomintang-controlled areas to that of a colonial country. Chiang Kai-shek sold the sovereign rights of China in return for American aid. In November 1946, the United States and Chiang Kai-shek concluded a Sino-American Treaty of Friendship, Trade and Navigation. With the signing of this treaty and other treaties and agreements, Chiang Kai-shek sold China's territorial, military, domestic, diplomatic and economic rights to the United States. From the time of the Japanese surrender up to July 1947, Chiang Kai-shek obtained American aid valued at more than 4,000 million U.S. dollars. American goods flooded the Kuomintang-controlled areas, and this, combined with the cruel exactions and plunder of the people committed by Chiang Kai-shek in order to wage his civil war, accelerated the development of an unparalleled economic crisis. Any hopes for the survival of industries and commerce owned by the national bourgeoisie were crushed. Agriculture was also on the brink of collapse. This fact, together with the soaring of commodity prices and currency inflation, made the life of the people almost unbearable. The prices of basic consumer goods, on the eve of the Japanese surrender, were 1,800 times above the pre-war level. By April 1947, they had risen 60,000 fold. The total note issue of the Chiang Kai-shek government on the eve of the War of Resistance was 1,400 million yuan. By the eve of the Japanese surrender it had mounted to 500,000 million yuan, and by April 1947, it had soared to over 16,000,000 million yuan.

The people's patriotic democratic movement gained impetus as the economic crisis deepened, while Chiang Kai-shek's political chicanery drifted towards bankruptcy and his military campaigns failed. The struggles of workers, students and the masses of people of all walks of life against U.S. imperialism and Chiang Kai-shek formed a second revolutionary front, working in co-ordination with the armed struggles of the military and civilian population in the Liberated Areas. In September 1946 the people of Shanghai launched a week of demonstrations under the slogan, "American Troops, Get Out of China!" On December 1, when Chiang Kai-shek's bogus National Assembly was in session, an incident occurred in Shanghai in which thousands of pavement stall-holders started a struggle for survival. When the scattered, individual stall-holders petitioned for their right to do business, they were subjected to wanton shootings by the Kuomintang military and police forces. At the end of December half a million students rose in protest following the rape of a Beijing University girl student by Americansoldiers. In May 1947 the students started another movement, this time in protest against hunger, persecution and civil war. Although Chiang Kai-shek resorted to arrest, imprisonment, beatings and shootings in an attempt to suppress the struggles of the students, workers and broad masses, the struggles became more resolute and fiercer than ever. In May 1948, another patriotic movement arose in protest against the fostering of a resurgence of Japanese militarism by the United States.

Chiang Kai-shek, who was bent on making himself an enemy of the people, found himself besieged by the people of the country. The people in the Kuomintang-controlled areas were suffering serious hardships and, centring all their hopes on the Communist Party, yearned for the early arrival of the People's Liberation Army.

After the People's Liberation Army shifted to strategic offensive, the people's democratic united front under the leadership of the Communist Party took on a more definite form. On October 10, 1947 the Chinese People's Liberation Army issued a manifesto, raising such slogans as "Overthrow Chiang Kai-shek and form a democratic coalition government". The manifesto advocated unity between workers, peasants, soldiers, intellectuals and businessmen, all oppressed classes, all people's organizations, democratic parties, ethnic minorities, overseas Chinese and other patriots; the formation of a national united front; the overthrow of the dictatorial Chiang Kai-shek government; and the establishment of a democratic coalition government. This manifesto roused those who were against the Chiang Kai-shek dictatorial government to rally under the leadership of the Chinese Communist Party and to form a people's democratic united front. On October 27 Chiang Kai-shek issued an order to dissolve the China Democratic League. Some bourgeois intellectuals who had hitherto entertained the illusion of steering a middle road between revolution and counter-revolution now realized that under the oppression of the Kuomintang reactionaries the third road was a bankrupt illusion.

After the dissolution of the China Democratic League, the various middle-of-the-road political groups were got together with the help of the Communist Party. In the spring of 1948 Shen Junru and other leaders of the Democratic League reestablished their leading organization in Hongkong. Several democratic organizations within the Kuomintang also joined forces and formed the Revolutionary Committee of the Kuomintang led by Li Jishen and He Xiangning. They advocated co-operation with the Communist Party and opposition to the reactionary policy of the Kuomintang and the U.S. policy of aggression. Other democratic parties, such as the Chinese Peasants' and Workers' Democratic Party, the China Association for Promoting Democracy, the China Democratic National Construction Association, and the Jiu San Society, and democrats without party affiliation also became more politically active. Conditions were ripe for the formation of a people's democratic united front led by the Chinese Communist Party and composed of all the democratic parties and people's organizations.

On International Labour Day, May 1, 1948, the Communist Party issued a call for the speedy convocation of a new People's Political Consultative Conference, from which all reactionary elements were to be excluded, and the establishment of a democratic coalition government. The call received the enthusiastic support of the people throughout the country, and democratic parties and many democratic persons issued circular telegrams warmly endorsing this proposal and pledging their support.

The Victory of the Third Revolutionary Civil War In the spring and summer of 1948 the People's Liberation Army successively attacked and captured a large number of heavily fortified and strongly defended cities and towns. After September 1948, it launched the three major campaigns of Liaoxi-Shenyang, Huai-Hai and Beiping-Tianjin. They were decisive battles between the main force of the People's Liberation Army and that of Chiang Kai-shek. In the Liaoxi-Shenyang campaign, which took place between September 12 and November 2, the Northeast People's Liberation Army wiped out the main force of the Kuomintang army in the Northeast, comprising 470,000 men, and liberated the whole of northeast China. The People's Liberation Army was now superior to Chiang Kai-shek's forces not only in quality but also in quantity. The Kuomintang's military strength had fallen to 2,900,000 men while that of the People's Liberation Army had risen to 3,000,000. In the Huai-Hai campaign, which took place between November 7, 1948 and January 10, 1949, the East China and Central Plains field armies, commanded by the General Front Committee, which included Liu Bocheng, Chen Yi, Su Yu and Tan Zhenlin, with Deng Xiaoping as secretary, put out of action the picked forces of the Kuomintang army in east China, totalling 550,000 men, in the Xuzhou-Suxian-Yongcheng area and liberated, with the exception of a few points, those parts of east China and the central plains areas north of the Changjiang River. Nanjing, the centre of Kuomintang reactionary rule, and Shanghai were thus left exposed to the People's Liberation Army. The Beiping-Tianjin campaign began on December 5, 1948 and concluded on January 31, 1949. The Kuomintang forces holding Tianjin and Zhangjiakou were wiped out and the Beiping garrison was peacefully reorganized. In this campaign the People's Liberation Army liquidated a part of the main force of the Kuomintang army totalling 520,000 men and liberated practically the whole of north China. The three major campaigns cost the Kuomintang army the greater part of its main force and enabled the

Chinese people's revolution to win a fundamental military victory.

In March 1949, following the victory of the revolution, the Communist Party convened the Second Plenary Session of the Seventh Central Committee. Under the guidance of Mao Zedong, the session decided to shift the centre of gravity of the Party's work from the countryside to the cities. It stressed the necessity for relying on the working class and for learning how to administer the cities. The conference studied and analysed the different sectors of China's economy, and pointed out the leading role of socialist state-owned economy in the national economy. It laid down a series of specific policies which the Party should adopt towards the various sectors of China's economy, and formulated the basic principles governing China's transition to socialism. After the close of this session the Central Committee of the Chinese Communist Party and the general headquarters of the People's Liberation Army were moved to Beijing.

The military situation was changing rapidly throughout the country in favour of the revolution. The collapse of Kuomintang reactionary rule was fast approaching. The Kuomintang ruling bloc, anxious to stave off defeat and acting on the direction of the United States, embarked on a "peace offensive". On January 1, 1949, Chiang Kai-shek advanced a hypocritical proposal pleading for "peace". It was an attempt to gain time in which to recuperate from the wounds of war, so that he might stage a "comeback" and destroy the revolution. Shortly afterwards, Chiang Kai-shek announced his "retirement" and let Vice-President Li Zongren cope with the situation while he manipulated from behind the scene. Mao Zedong answered this plea with a statement on January 14, putting forward eight conditions for the realization of a genuine peace. Delegates of the Communist Party and representatives of the Kuomintang's Li Zongren government drew up an Agreement on Internal Peace, but after fifteen days of negotiation the Kuomintang government, on April 20, 1949, refused to sign it. This completely exposed the hypocritical nature of the "peace offensive" of the Kuomintang.

The People's Liberation Army began to cross the Changjiang River the next day, April 21, and advanced towards areas south of the river to complete its mission of the liberation of the country. Two days later, Nanjing, the centre of Kuomintang reactionary rule, was liberated, thus formally ending that rule. This was immediately followed by a sweeping advance of the People's Liberation Army on a battle front extending for thousands of li from south of Changjiang to northwest China. In the course of this advance the remnants of Chiang Kai-shek's forces were rooted out and defeated, and by the end of 1949, the whole of the mainland, with the exception of Tibet, was liberated. A basic victory was achieved in the revolutionary war of the Chinese people throughout the country.

Between July 1946 and June 1950, the Chinese People's Liberation Army put out of action more than 8,070,000 men of the Kuomintang's armed forces, captured more than 54,400 artillery pieces, 319,900 machine-guns, 1,000 tanks and armoured cars, 20,000 motor vehicles, and large quantities of other arms and equipment.

The Opening of the Chinese People's Political Consultative Conference After the overthrow of the reactionary rule of the Kuomintang throughout the country, the Chinese people set about establishing their own state. Mao

Zedong, on July 1, 1949, published an article entitled *On the People's Democratic Dictatorship,* explaining the nature and character of the state in the new China, and the basic policies on which it would be based. In it, he pointed out that the People's Republic of China is a "people's democratic dictatorship under the leadership of the working class (through the Communist Party) and based upon the alliance of workers and peasants". He also stated that in matters of foreign policy China "must unite as one with the international revolutionary forces".[1] In this work, Mao Zedong, on behalf of the Party Central Committee, laid down the basic principles governing the construction of New China.

On September 21, the First Plenary Session of the Chinese People's Political Consultative Conference opened in Beijing. It was a conference of the people's democratic united front led by the working class and based on the alliance of workers and peasants. It included representatives of workers, peasants, the petty bourgeoisie, the national bourgeoisie, other democratic patriotic elements, the people of the ethnic minorities and overseas Chinese. The Chinese People's Political Consultative Conference was representative of the people of the whole country. Hence, though it was not elected on the basis of universal suffrage, it did, in fact, represent the will of the people of the whole country. Pending the convocation of a National People's Congress, it exercised the functions of such a body. Following a discussion on the draft proposals submitted by the Communist Party, the Conference adopted the Common Programme of the Chinese People's

---

[1] *Selected Works of Mao Zedong,* Foreign Languages Press, Beijing, 1977, Vol. IV, p. 422.

Political Consultative Conference. This programme defined the character and tasks of the new China, the rights and duties of the people, and the fundamental principles governing the structure of the new state power, its military system, and the economic, cultural, educational, and foreign policies of the new state as well as its policy on ethnic minorities. The programme clearly laid down the leading political position of the working class and the leading position of the socialist sector of the economy in the economy of the nation, thus providing an important guarantee for the transition of the People's Republic of China towards socialism. The Common Programme became the Chinese people's great provisional charter. The conference also passed the Organic Law of the Chinese People's Political Consultative Conference, and the Organic Law of the Central People's Government of the People's Republic of China. It elected Mao Zedong as Chairman of the Central People's Government Council; Zhu De, Liu Shaoqi, Soong Ching Ling, Li Jishen, Zhang Lan and Gao Gang as Vice-Chairman; and Zhou Enlai and 55 others as members of the Central People's Government Council. The conference also decided on a national flag and a national anthem and chose Beijing as the capital of the country.

The Establishment of the People's Republic of China

Grand ceremonies inaugurating the People's Republic of China were held in Beijing on October 1, 1949. From Tian An Men in Beijing, Mao Zedong issued a proclamation to the people of the country and to the entire world, solemnly declaring the establishment of the People's Republic of China and the Central People's Government. This marked the opening of a new epoch in China's history. Starting from the May 4th Movement of 1919, the Chinese people's new democratic revolution against imperialism, feudalism and bureaucrat-capitalism had passed through thirty years of struggle. During those years it had lost countless revolutionary martyrs and undergone many intense trials and tribulations. The revolution had finally triumphed under the correct leadership of the Chinese Communist Party. This victory was a triumph for Marxism-Leninism in China, with a population of 600 million. It was a new triumph for Marxism-Leninism in a colonial and semi-colonial country. It was a great triumph for the cause of world peace, democracy and socialism.

Mao Zedong had pointed out as early as 1940 in his article *On New Democracy*: ". . . it follows from the colonial, semi-colonial and semi-feudal character of present-day Chinese society that the Chinese revolution must be divided into two stages. The first step is to change the colonial, semi-colonial and semi-feudal form of society into an independent, democratic society. The second is to carry the revolution forward and build a socialist society."[1]

The establishment of the People's Republic of China marked the completion of the first step of the Chinese revolution and the commencement of the second. It began a new epoch in China's history, the great epoch of transition to socialism under the people's democratic dictatorship. The Chinese Communist Party is the leading political party in the People's Republic of China. It has assumed the historic mission of leading the socialist transformation and socialist construction of China.

---

[1] *Selected Works of Mao Zedong,* Foreign Languages Press, Beijing, 1975, Vol. II, p. 342.

V. THE CONTEMPORARY CULTURAL AND IDEOLOGICAL REVOLUTION IN CHINA

On China's cultural and ideological front, the period preceding the May 4th Movement and the period following it form two distinct epochs. Before the May 4th Movement, the struggle on China's cultural front was a struggle between the new culture (New Learning) of the bourgeoisie and the old culture (Old Learning) of the feudal landlord class. After the May 4th Movement, things changed. A fresh and completely new cultural force appeared in China — the communist cultural ideology, that is, the communist world outlook and Marxist-Leninist theory of social revolution.

The new democratic revolution was a people's revolution led by the working class through the Chinese Communist Party. It was based on the alliance of workers and peasants, and was directed against imperialism, feudalism and bureaucrat-capitalism. The new democratic cultural revolution, led and inspired by the communist cultural ideology, was also anti-feudal, anti-comprador and anti-fascist in character.

During the period of the old democratic revolution the New Learning school, which represented the cultural ideology of the bourgeoisie, combated the reactionary cultural alliance of feudal and comprador ideology, and it was defeated. After its defeat, the New Learning school split. One group was active in demanding democracy and science, another group wavered, unable to decide which way to go, yet another group watched to see whether there was any opportunity which might be turned to their advantage. The rest came to terms or united with the reactionary cultural alliance. The reactionary cultural alliance, which was dominated by imperialist culture, gained in influence with the support of the degenerate elements of the New Learning school. It became the main force in the cultural world of the time, and as such was the principal target of the new democratic cultural revolution.

The victory of the Great October Socialist Revolution in Russia brought the Chinese people new hopes of national liberation. The May 4th Movement broke out in 1919, and the Chinese people's revolution entered a new historical epoch.

The May 4th Movement was both an anti-imperialist and an anti-feudal movement. In the beginning it was a revolutionary movement of the united front of three sections of the people — the intellectuals with a rudimentary communist ideology, the revolutionary petty-bourgeois intellectuals, and the bourgeois intellectuals. The latter made up the right wing of the movement at that time. The three groups were originally members of the New Learning school, who had wavered at the crossroads and adopted a wait-and-see attitude. The most advanced section of them broke away from the old democratic ideas that bound them, accepted the rudiments of communism and as a result took a leading position in this great movement. Tested and tempered by practical experience in the struggle, they ideologically and organizationally prepared the way for the founding of the Chinese Communist Party in 1921.

The May 4th Movement, led by the intellectuals with a rudimentary communist ideology, promoted science and democracy, opposed Confucianism, the old ethical code, the old literature, superstition and the entire old social-political system. Displaying the thorough-going revolutionary spirit of the Chinese people, Li Dazhao in his *Youth* urged the young people to "smash the trammels of the past and destroy the yoke of the old teachings" to create a democratic "young China". The *Call to Arms* by Lu Xun and *The Goddess* by Guo Moruo resounded with the militant call for uncompromising struggle against feudalism. The hammer blows of the new cultural movement battered down the bastion of the old ethics, Confucianism, and pounded heavily on the old culture. This was the greatest and most thorough-going cultural revolution since the dawn of Chinese history.

After the founding of the Chinese Communist Party, the Chinese people's revolution deepened, and the cultural struggle and the political struggle likewise sharpened. The great majority of the bourgeois intellectuals who constituted the right wing of the May 4th Movement, went over to the reactionary cultural alliance, and under the direction of the imperialists, were used as tools against the new democratic culture. Hu Shi was a particularly useful tool of the reactionaries.

The new cultural force led by the Chinese Communist Party united with all those allies that could be united and launched heroic attacks on the imperialist and feudal culture. It made great strides in the domain of the social sciences and of the arts and letters, including philosophy, economics, political science, military science, history, literature and art — the theatre, the cinema, music, sculpture and painting. This new cultural force created a great revolution in both ideological content and form, as for example in the written language. Its influence was great, its power invincible. The scope of its development is unparalleled in Chinese history. Lu Xun was the greatest and the most militant standard-bearer of this new cultural force. In the early twenties, the Creation Society headed by Guo Moruo and Cheng Fangwu began to explore the Marxist theory on literature and art. In the late twenties, Lu Xun and other revolutionary writers avidly studied and propagated the Marxist theory on literature and art, pushing forward the movement for proletarian literature and art. In March 1930, with the leadership and support of the Communist Party, Lu Xun and other revolutionary writers initiated and founded the League of Left-Wing Writers. The League encouraged the writers to disseminate Marxism-Leninism, work hard at creative writing and gear their work to the needs of the current revolutionary struggle, making contributions to both literary theory and creative writing. Many Marxist-Leninist works were translated into Chinese and new sociological works gained in popularity. With convincing arguments, Guo Moruo in his *Study of Ancient Chinese Society* proved the development of ancient Chinese society as being wholly consistent with the universal law governing social development as revealed by Marx and Engels. Thus Guo Moruo knocked the bottom out of Hu Shi and company's fallacies that the situation in China was different and that Marxism did not apply to China. The reactionary cultural alliance, with Hu Shi as its chief, was routed before the onslaughts of the new cultural force.

In its cultural tyranny the Kuomintang resorted to repressive measures and terrorist policies. As Lu Xun said, "Slander, suppression, imprisonment and slaughter are being used to resist Left-wing art and literature, and hooligans, spies, stool-pigeons and butchers are against

Left-wing writers." Defying the Kuomintang's cultural suppression, he voiced his wrath in his pungent essays that reflected the soul of China's millions and exposed the ugly features of the dark forces. His caustic pen "is a gun against imperialists, traitors, warlords, bureaucrats, local tyrants, bad gentry, fascists and all other monsters, and a detector revealing them for what they are" (Statement in Mourning for Lu Xun to the People of China and the World by the Central Committee of the Chinese Communist Party and the Soviet Republic of the Chinese People). Lu Xun's essays enlightened and inspired the people and pointed out the way forward for them. Qu Qiubai, who worked with Lu Xun for the promotion of left-wing culture, also wrote many militant essays and literary reviews. *Midnight,* a novel by Mao Dun, brought both the comprador and national capitalists to life and showed why capitalism meant an impasse for semi-colonial, semi-feudal China. The Kuomintang's cultural suppression suffered an ignominious defeat and the new cultural force won a complete victory.

Mao Zedong, the great inheritor of the best of ancient Chinese culture and founder of the new culture, brilliantly summed up the history of modern Chinese culture and clearly indicated the way for the forward march of the new cultural force.

In January 1940 Mao Zedong published his *On New Democracy.* In it he analysed the bourgeois culture of the period of the old democratic revolution and the proletarian culture of the period of the new democratic revolution. He explained why bourgeois culture would inevitably fail and demonstrated the invincibility of proletarian culture. He pointed out that the new culture must be national, scientific and popular in character, being both anti-imperialist and anti-feudal. *On New Democracy* opened the way for an unlimited development of Chinese culture.

In May 1942 Mao Zedong published his *Talks at the Yanan Forum on Literature and Art.* In this celebrated work he criticized the various wrong conceptions of the non-proletarian, mainly petty-bourgeois intellectuals, in regard to literature and art. He explained many fundamental questions on the theory of literature and art, and clearly pointed out the general direction in which literature and art should be made to serve the workers, peasants and soldiers. This work is an important contribution to Marxist theory as applied to literature and art.

Mao Zedong published his work *On the People's Democratic Dictatorship* on July 1, 1949, in commemoration of the 28th anniversary of the founding of the Chinese Communist Party. It gave a brief but penetrating summary of the development of Chinese culture since 1840. This article pointed out:

> All other ways have been tried and failed. Of the people who hankered after those ways, some have fallen, some have awakened and some are changing their ideas. Events are developing so swiftly that many feel the abruptness of change and the need to learn anew. This state of mind is understandable and we welcome this worthy desire to learn anew.[1]

"All other ways" was a reference to the so-called New Learning acquired by Chinese intellectuals from the

---

[1] *Selected Works of Mao Zedong*, Foreign Languages Press, Beijing, 1977, Vol. IV, p. 414.

Western capitalist states following the Opium War. As a result of the victory of the new democratic revolution — the victory of Marxism-Leninism in China — "Western bourgeois civilization, bourgeois democracy and the plan for a bourgeois republic have all gone bankrupt in the eyes of the Chinese people",[1] and the social theories of the New Learning proved to be entirely useless. The degenerate section of the New Learning school who had always been hostile towards the new democratic culture, were willing to serve as cultural lackeys of imperialism. An overwhelming majority of the New Learning school were patriots at heart. Their demand to learn the theories of Marxism-Leninism arose quite naturally. They remoulded their ideology on this basis, strove to cleanse themselves of their bourgeois ideology and embraced working-class ideology step by step. This signified that the big cultural force would expand its membership and that the study of natural and social sciences and the creative work in the field of literature and art would be further developed and strengthened.

China is a country which has one of the most ancient civilizations and a recorded history of nearly four thousand years. Annals of ancient civilization record a well-developed agriculture and handicraft industry. They also show the existence of many great thinkers, scientists, inventors, statesmen, military scientists, men of letters, and artists. This is shown by the wealth of cultural works still in existence. Present-day culture has evolved and is being developed from the culture of ancient times. The rich legacy of China's old culture provides a favour-

---

[1] *Ibid.*

able basis for the development of the new culture. The main thing is to indefatigably study the Marxist-Leninist point of view and method, and earnestly re-evaluate the cultural heritage, eliminating the chaff and absorbing the essence, and making it a part of the useful knowledge with which to enrich the minds of the Chinese people. Cultural workers in China treasure their cultural heritage and are turning it to good account.

POSTSCRIPT

In 1951, the Chinese Historical Society decided to compile a book giving a brief introduction to Chinese history to meet the needs of readers at home and abroad. For this purpose, Guo Moruo and Fan Wenlan, President and Vice-President respectively of the Society, called a meeting attended by ten or more historians, at which it was decided that the book was to be entitled *Concise History of China* and that it was to embrace the viewpoints of the majority of researchers in Chinese history. Jian Bozan (1898-1968), then social science professor of Yenching University and, from 1952, head of the Department of History of Beijing University, Shao Xunzheng (1909-73), then head of the Department of History of Qinghua University, and myself were chosen as the writers. Fan Wenlan gave consistent guidance to the discussion, revision and finalization of the book. The book was published by the People's Publishing House in February 1956 and reprinted several times. It was published in English, German and French by the Foreign Languages Press, and in Korean, Uygur and Kazak by the Nationality Publishing House.

During the ten disastrous years of 1966-76, *Concise History of China* came under fire and the two veteran historians, Jian Bozan and Shao Xunzheng, died as a result of persecution. The book is being republished at a time when historical research is being revived in China.

Some changes have been made before the book was reprinted. The part about the early period of Chinese history, which had been carefully revised by Professor Jian Bozan himself, was collated by Zhang Chuanxi; the modern part was revised by Chen Qinghua and the contemporary part by myself.

Hu Hua

November 22, 1979

INDEX

中国历史概要
翦伯赞 邵循正 胡华 编著
*
外文出版社出版
（中国北京百万庄路24号）
外文印刷厂印刷
中国国际书店发行
1964年（32开）第一版
1981年 第二版
编号：（英）11050—26
00150
11—E—612P